Praise for

Silent Echoes

Discovering Early Hollywood Through the Films of Buster Keaton

"MIND-BOGGLING . . . What John Bengtson has done is nothing short of remarkable: a deft combination of detective work, archeology, and film buffery. I can't get enough of it!" —LEONARD MALTIN, film critic and historian

"This is a cinematic and photographic detective story of the first order. Time and artifice have been stripped away. What's left is a wonderful portrait of a city, its principal industry, and one of its best artists."
—KEN BURNS, author/director, *The Civil War, Baseball, Jazz,* etc.

"Bengtson captures the same eerie feeling I sometimes get when watching Keaton, who is the greatest of the silent clowns: The sense that Buster occupies not the fantasy world of many silent comedies, but a real world right down the street from our own." —ROGER EBERT, film critic and historian

"A new art form."
—KEVIN BROWNLOW, director and film historian

"[A] Proustian collage of time and memory, biography and history, urban growth and artistic expression."
—DAVE KEHR, *New York Times*

"Astonishing is a mild word for what John Bengtson has accomplished . . . this book is something like a miracle."
—KENNETH TURAN, film critic, *Los Angeles Times*

"The book is meticulous. It's ingenious. It's inexhaustibly fascinating . . . the feeling evoked is not one of nostalgia—of seeking the past in the present—but the opposite, of finding the present in the past. It's disconcerting, vaguely romantic and hard to define. But it has a way of keeping *Silent Echoes* by the bedside for a long time."
—MICK LASALLE, *San Francisco Chronicle*

"A remarkable piece of detective work."
—CHARLES CHAMPLIN, author of *Hollywood's Revolutionary Decade*

"A terrifically resourceful work of pictorial scholarship that rewinds time's projector. A fascinating work of film history in which, to quote film historian Kevin Brownlow, 'he may have invented a new art form' . . . Bengtson's enthusiasm for his subject is contagious . . . Like collaborations between Eadweard Muybridge and David Hockney . . . His inventive and intriguing work is a kind of deconstructed poem, a visual ode to a world that's vanished yet present."

—TOM NOLAN, *San Francisco Chronicle Book Review*

"BRILLIANT. [An] utterly winning book that can be used and enjoyed as a filmography of Buster Keaton, a work of architectural history, urban geography and popular culture, and a kind of scavenger hunt that invites us to search out the relics and artifacts of old Hollywood.

Silent Echoes . . . exerts a strong and sometimes almost hypnotic allure of its own [that] carries us back and forth in time. [R]eading Bengtson's book is like recalling a dimly remembered dream, sometimes delightful and sometimes disturbing, but always rich in meaning."

—JONATHAN KIRSCH, *Los Angeles Times*

"The most complete work on film locations that has ever been published. Any student of early filmmaking in Los Angeles—not to mention Keaton fans—will find this elegant volume to be indispensable."

—*American Cinematographer*

"It is only fair to warn true lovers of Hollywood history—not to mention Keaton fans—that we will fall into the contents of this incredible book like Alice down the rabbit hole. Chores will go undone as we pore over its archival photos, diagrams, maps, explanations and addresses til we jump in our cars to search out whatever blessedly still-standing sites we can find. In discussing/showing the spots and shots where Keaton made his movies, John Bengtson extensively demonstrates what Kevin Brownlow calls "a new art form." Not only will Bengtson's years of remarkable sleuthing give greater meaning to familiar Hollywood neighborhoods, it will sweetly enhance our viewing of Keaton's films for the rest of our lives."

—LISA MITCHELL, *DGA Magazine, Directors Guild of America*

"*Silent Echoes* is a conversation piece indeed. I'm grabbing people and showing them this one . . . you must buy this landmark book."

—*The Keaton Chronicle*

"The then-and-now photo comparisons are captivating, but Bengtson goes further, offering aerial photographs and maps and vastly entertaining on-the-set photos of Keaton and crew at work . . . . For fans of both Keaton and Los Angeles, it's essential reading."

—ROBERT W. BUTLER, *Kansas City Star*

"A MIRACLE. Entertaining, enlightening, and innovative. . . . Bengtson has rewritten film history and recreated the world of Buster Keaton—Los Angeles in the 1920s—before our unbelieving eyes." —Piet Schreuders, *Furore Magazine*

Silent Traces

Discovering Early Hollywood Through the Films of Charlie Chaplin

John Bengtson
Foreword by **Kevin Brownlow**

SANTA
MONICA
PRESS

Published by: Santa Monica Press LLC
P.O. Box 1076
Santa Monica, CA 90406-1076
1-800-784-9553
www.santamonicapress.com
books@santamonicapress.com

Printed in the United States

Santa Monica Press books are available at special quantity discounts when purchased in bulk by corporations, organizations, or groups. Please call our Special Sales department at 1-800-784-9553.

ISBN 1-59580-014-X

Library of Congress Cataloging-in-Publication Data

Bengtson, John, 1957-
  Silent traces : discovering early Hollywood through the films of Charlie Chaplin / by John Bengtson.
    p. cm.
  ISBN 1-59580-014-X
  1. Chaplin, Charlie, 1889-1977--Criticism and interpretation. 2. Motion picture locations--California. I. Title.

PN2287.C5B35 2006
791.4302'8092--dc21
  [B]

Cover and interior design and production by Future Studio

Contents

Dedication

With love and gratitude to my mother Edla Bengtson,
and the memory of my father Andy Bengtson,
whose unconditional love and support sustain me still.

Acknowledgments

This book was truly a collaborative effort. Without minimizing my gratitude to all who have assisted, these eight colleagues were especially generous in sharing their expertise, discoveries, and enthusiasm:

Paul R. Ayers is an attorney, historian, and archivist who made many discoveries and who also assisted with my Buster Keaton book *Silent Echoes*.

Jeffrey Castel De Oro is a visual effects artist and vintage film enthusiast who took a majority of the contemporary photos, and who also greatly assisted with *Silent Echoes*.

William D. Estrada is Curator of California and American History of the Natural History Museum of Los Angeles County, and author of *Los Angeles's Olvera Street* (Arcadia, 2006).

David Kiehn is Historian for the Niles Essanay Silent Film Museum, and is author of *Broncho Billy Anderson and the Essanay Film Company* (Farwell Press, 2003).

Gerald Smith is a Chaplin enthusiast whose wonderful Chaplin Film Locations THEN & NOW website (http://jerre.com) was the starting point for many discoveries in this book. A recently retired IBM electrical engineer, Gerald devotes time to his new passion of making THEN & NOW films.

Christopher Snowden is a film historian and archivist, and as proprietor of Unknown Video sells vintage films at http://www.unknownvideo.com.

David Totheroh is a cabinetmaker who has lived the past 35 years on the Topanga Canyon property owned by his grandfather, Chaplin cameraman Rollie Totheroh, and who seeks to study and honor his grandfather's contributions to Chaplin's work.

Brent Walker is a film historian and freelance writer for Turner Classic Movies, and author of *Mack Sennett's Fun Factory*.

I would also like to give my special thanks to the following persons who contributed so much to the creation of this book.

To Kate Guyonvarch of Association Chaplin; David Shepard of Film Preservation Associates; Gary Dartnall and Tim Lanza of the Douris Corporation; Suzanne Lloyd and Chuck Johnson of Harold Lloyd Entertainment, Inc.; Serge Bromberg of Lobster Films; Paul E. Gierucki and William Hunt of Laughsmith Entertainment Inc.; Larry Stefan, Paul Lisy, and Richard M. Roberts of the Slaphappy Collection; Jeffrey Vance; and Kevin Brownlow for their generous support.

To Carolyn Cole and Robert Anderson of the Los Angeles Public Library; Dace Taube of the USC Regional History Center, Special Collection; Marc Wanamaker of Bison Archives; and John M. Cahoon, Collections Manager, Seaver Center for Western History Research, Natural History Museum of Los Angeles County.

To Lisa Henson and Suzanne Koenig of The Jim Henson Company.

To web designer extraordinaire, Victoria Sainte-Claire, at http://www.cybertints.com/.

To Doug Sulpy; Snowden Becker, Public Access Coordinator Academy Film Archive; Serge Bromberg of Lobster Films; Davide Pozzi of Cineteca di Bologna; and the British Film Institute for assistance with frame captures from the Keystone films.

For generously sharing information and photographs: Steve Vaught; Brent Dickerson; Dr. Lisa Stein; Marilyn Slater; Bonnie McCourt; Bruce Torrence; Martin Schall; David Sameth; Bryant Arnett; Jeff Stanton; Sam Gill; Jill M. Singleton and Philip Holmes; Tim Lussier of www.SilentsAreGolden.com; Harry Medved; Robert S. Birchard; Elizabeth Foote; David Raptka; Shelly Roberts and Shunichi Ohkubo; Kenneth & Gabrielle Adelman of California Coastal Records; Mary Sue Roberts; Bill Roddy of http://americahurrah.com/; Stephen Loo; Bruce Bengtson; June Ahn; Professor Jan Lin and College Archivist Jean Paule of Occidental College; Russ Davies; Matthew Roth; Charles Seims; Kristin York of the Sugar Bowl Ski Resort; Norm Sayler at Donner Ski Ranch; and Dana Scanlon.

And to my wife Kristin and daughters Linden, Arden, and McKenna, for their love and support.

Foreword

I was watching a silent film the other day which had been shot in the streets of South London in 1922. Those same streets would be flattened 18 years later in the Blitz. Yet there was something remarkably familiar about them. Of course! They were the same streets Chaplin had re-created in his films. Instead of London, Chaplin made his pictures in sunny and somnolent Hollywood, less like South London than almost any town you can imagine. Even so, his set designer supplied the treeless terraces, the brick walls, the bollards, and the arched alleyways that could only be South London or the East End.

Chaplin retained British citizenship all his life, to the irritation of nationalistic Americans, and remained a Londoner, too, although why he should have fond memories after the wretched experiences he and his brother were put through, I cannot imagine. Whenever he came to London, he went on nostalgic walks. (You can see home movies shot in Lambeth by Oona Chaplin on the Warner Bros. DVD of *Limelight.*)

Earlier this year, I was taken on a tour of South London by Chaplin expert Tony Merrick and I was astonished at how much still survives from Chaplin's era. One of the most touching moments I experienced was when I was shown the railings of Kennington Park, reproduced on the backlot in *City Lights*, where the blind girl sells Charlie the flower. You ignore it until it's pointed out to you and then there is no doubt, despite the busy traffic and the nearby underground station.

The most astonishing discovery came when Tony took us into a working man's club, sandwiched between Georgian terraces. He had a word with the man behind the bar and took us up some steps, through the kind of cobwebbed corridor you see in Universal horror films, and into a small Edwardian theatre, gaslights intact. It was due to be demolished—you could smell the mildew—but it was a wonderful surprise. A theatre, we were told, where the young Charlie and his brother Syd had almost certainly performed.

Chaplin often chose his locations because they reminded him of London. The forbidding institution from which Edna Purviance emerges with her baby in *The Kid* always suggested to me the workhouse where the Chaplins were incarcerated. It is just the sort of place you'd imagine Los Angeles tearing down and it is thrilling to discover, thanks to John Bengtson, that it still exists.

Chinatown hardly suggests London, and yet, as we now have a Chinatown in Soho, so too did we once have a Chinatown in Limehouse, on the river. You can see it reproduced in *Broken Blossoms* (1919), for which D.W. Griffith combined studio sets with parts of the Los Angeles Chinatown—the same parts Chaplin uses in *The Kid* and in *Caught in a Cabaret*. That whole area has been scoured clean off the map and the district around the railroad station has lost all its atmosphere.

Los Angeles must be the fastest changing city in the world. When I first visited it in 1964, film people were bemoaning the loss of the D. W. Griffith studio—it had become, somewhat unromantically, a supermarket—and the fact that the Keystone studios had been virtually eliminated. I was taken on a tour of Sennett locations by one of Chaplin's first leading ladies, Minta Durfee, who had married Roscoe Arbuckle. She found very little left. Forty years later, had it not been for John Bengtson's heroic researches, virtually all traces of the silent era would likely have been erased.

But look what he's discovered!

While spectacular architectural follies, like the Hollywood Hotel or the Bradbury Mansion, have long since gone, he shows us that the firehouse where Charlie—nearly a century ago—shot *The Fireman* is still standing, as a Korean bridal shop.

What a debt we owe him! Bengtson's sense of observation is so acute that he can recognize a wall which has undergone enough changes to make it unrecognizable to the rest of us. Sadly, developers do not share the same sense of history as he does. I was filming on the backlot of a Hollywood studio recently, and wanted to use glass stages from the silent era as a background. "Don't show those," said the studio manager. "People might stop us tearing them down."

KEVIN BROWNLOW
London, England

Introduction

During the opening days of 1914, a young English music hall entertainer named Charles Spencer Chaplin stepped in front of a motion picture camera for the first time. He did so in a special place, in the heart of Downtown Los Angeles. Chaplin's earliest scenes were filmed amid the bustling trolley cars and horse drawn wagons at First and Broadway, by the corner of the Los Angeles Times Building (newly rebuilt from a terrorist bombing), and in the shadow of Court Hill nearby. Postcards at the time proudly hailed Broadway as "the best lighted street in the world," lined with stately civic buildings such as the Romanesque City Hall and the towering sandstone L.A. County Courthouse, both built in the late 1880s.

From these heady early days, Chaplin and Los Angeles would both undergo tremendous change. In a few short months, the modestly successful actor would become the most famous entertainer on Earth, the world's first modern age superstar. At the same time, newly constructed aqueducts began drenching Los Angeles with imported water, spurring Los Angeles to bypass San Francisco as California's most populous region. The subsequent automobile boom and resulting explosive suburban growth would forever define L.A.'s contours in asphalt and concrete.

Chaplin played the Little Tramp, the underdog outsider forever looking in. Themes of alienation and adversity resonate throughout his films. In a 1922 *Vanity Fair* article publicizing *The Kid*, Chaplin describes the tale as taking place on London's weary East End streets, where Charlie had spent his youth in hardship and deprivation. Although not located in London, the real streets seen in the film had witnessed sufficient heartache to qualify as a dramatic setting in their own right. Chaplin filmed many scenes near the old Plaza de Los Angeles, where Hispanic descendants from California's former ruling class would find themselves ostracized in their own land, and in the old Chinatown nearby, where restrictive laws and immigration policies conspired to keep the descendants of Chinese railroad laborers on the lowest rung of the social and economic ladder. Perhaps intuitively, perhaps by design, Chaplin's themes of alienation echo from the very bricks and stones of the settings where he chose to shoot his films.

We would never be able to appreciate this subtle interplay of history and drama without first knowing where Chaplin shot his films.

So much has changed since 1914. The dusty roads and rural settings from Chaplin's earliest shorts soon gave way to the factories and paved highways appearing in films such as *Modern Times*. Hollywood's agricultural economy succumbed irresistibly to urban encroachment, hastened in part by the construction of Chaplin's own studio upon a former lemon grove. And on Broadway today, not only have the trolleys and many romantic buildings long since disappeared, but Court Hill itself has completely vanished. Once a hilltop island of Victorian mansions, sitting high above downtown, Court Hill and its charms have been completely obliterated—graded flat and hauled away one truckload at a time. Remarkably, the site where Chaplin once filmed on Court Hill beside the former Bradbury mansion now sits several stories up in the air above the current street level!

Because Chaplin shot so often on location, his films not only tell a story, they also capture a real time and place, recording history itself. While each scene provides a rare glimpse of the past, together they reveal, like the tiles of a mosaic, a clear picture of the real world in which Chaplin and the other silent-era comedians once filmed. With a little detective work, and a little imagination, we can use Chaplin's films as a portal to the past. We can explore the early Hollywood where Chaplin once worked, and the silent traces that remain today.

JOHN BENGTSON
Walnut Creek, California

Looking north up Broadway from Third Street past the former City Hall, circa early 1920s.

(For author tips on visiting Chaplin sites online, see Afterword, page 298.)

Southern California in 1920, before the freeways and urban sprawl. Chaplin filmed scenes in Chicago, in San Francisco, Oakland, Niles, and Truckee in Northern California, near Palmdale, and in Malibu, Santa Monica, Venice, Beverly Hills, Hollywood, Woodland Hills, Glendale, Pasadena, Arcadia (near Monrovia), Chinatown, Downtown Los Angeles, San Pedro, Wilmington, and Terminal Island (near Long Beach) in Southern California.

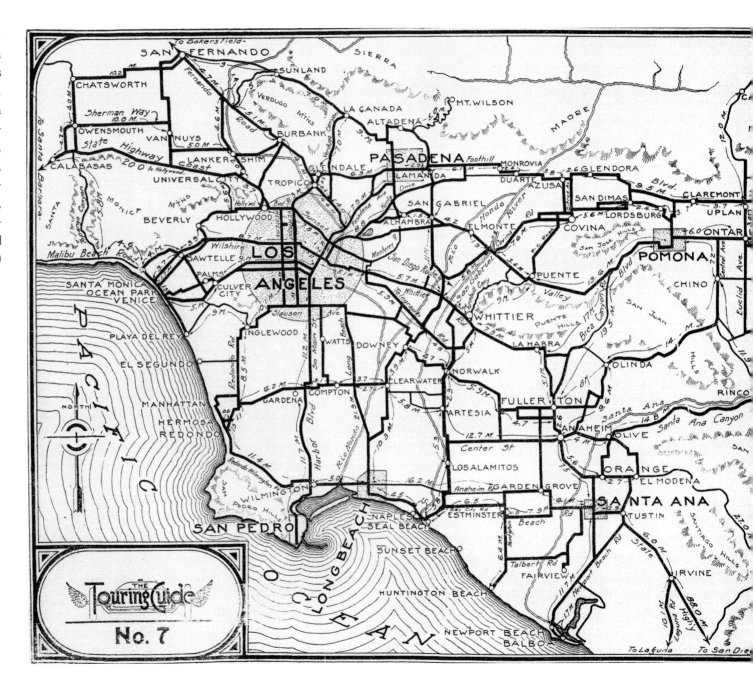

Plaza-Chinatown Overview

This 1933 aerial view looks north at the Plaza de Los Angeles and the former Chinatown, two of Chaplin's favorite places to film. The intersecting diagonal streets are Main (*left*) and Alameda (*right*).

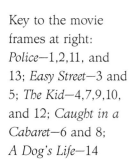

Key to the movie frames at right:
Police—1,2,11, and 13; *Easy Street*—3 and 5; *The Kid*—4,7,9,10, and 12; *Caught in a Cabaret*—6 and 8; *A Dog's Life*—14

The Keystone Studio

Born April 16, 1889, Charles Spencer Chaplin spent a harrowing childhood in London enduring great poverty and hardship before finding work on the stage as a juvenile lead. He graduated to the Fred Karno comedy troupe in 1908 when he was still 18. By the time Chaplin arrived for a second United States tour with the Karno company in October 1912, he was already, at age 23, a seasoned music hall performer.

In August of that same year, Adam Kessel and Charles Bauman founded The Keystone Film Co., the first studio dedicated solely to producing comedy films. Headed by Mack Sennett, a disciple of legendary director D.W. Griffith, the studio was home to such early comedy stars as Ford Sterling, Mabel Normand, and Roscoe "Fatty" Arbuckle, and became well-known for Sennett's "Bathing Beauties" and the slapstick antics of the Keystone Kops. Located at 1712 Allesandro Street (now Glendale Avenue) in the Edendale District of Los Angeles, the main filming stage still stands today, used as a public storage warehouse.

Legend has it that Sennett witnessed Chaplin's act in New York, and later sent a telegram to Karno inquiring about a man named "Chaffin, or something like that." Chaplin was performing in Portland, Oregon, when he signed the Keystone contract in September 1913 at $150 per week, double his music hall salary. Chaplin gave his final performance for Karno in Kansas City, and moved to Los Angeles that December. Following the holidays, Chaplin reported for work at the Keystone Studio on Monday, January 5, 1914. It was here that Chaplin stepped in front of the camera for the first time, and into history.

Kid Auto Races at Venice

Released February 7, 1914

In less than a year Chaplin would make 35 films for the Keystone Studio. Although *Kid Auto Races at Venice* was Chaplin's second motion picture, it seems fitting to lead off with it here, as it records the Little Tramp's first appearance on film. *Kid Auto* was filmed at the Junior Vanderbilt Cup Race held in Venice, California on Saturday, January 10, 1914, and at the children's pushmobile race held there the following day. The weekend shoot capped Chaplin's first week on the job at the Keystone Studio.

 Kid Auto depicts real events, with the simple "plot" involving camera-hound Charlie disturbing actors portraying newsreel cameramen attempting to record the races. Los Angeles car racing began in 1908 at a track near Playa del Rey, and came of age when philanthropist William K. Vanderbilt established the eponymous race in 1912. Building and racing gravity-powered pushmobile cars remains a popular Boy Scout activity to this day.

Venice
2 Big Days
Saturday
Jan. 10
Junior Vanderbilt Cup
Races
30 Entries 2:30 P.M.
Sunday
Jan. 11
2 Annual Prize
Pushmobile Parade 2:30 P.M.
60 Entries
Barney Oldfield, Teddy Tetzlaff
Earl Cooper—Judges
Be a Boy Again

This panning shot was filmed looking towards the southeast corner of Second (now Main) and Westminster in Venice. During the shot, children ride their pushmobiles down the gravity ramp in the background. In the far background is the Race Thru the Clouds (1911–1924), the first twin-track racing roller coaster built on the West Coast. Each track was nearly 4,000 feet long. The coaster sat beside a man-made lagoon situated at the end of Windward Avenue *(above right)*. Considering that in a few short months Chaplin would become an international celebrity, it is interesting to note that even in his debut appearance he seems to have completely captivated the audience watching him perform.

This view *(right)* replicates the panorama on the previous page. The vintage garage standing at the southeast corner of Second (Main) and Westminster was built later in 1914, after the time of filming. Because the garage was not present at the time, the homes and apartments behind it appear in the movie. The ellipse in the movie frame and photo *(below)* identify the same apartment building located at 212 San Juan Street. At the time, San Juan was not a paved street, but an ocean water channel named the Venus Canal. The arrow points to the Second Ave. street sign.

The Venice of America beach resort was built on reclaimed marshland by developer Abbott Kinney starting in 1904. The planned community was situated on eight miles of man-made canals, radiating from a large central lagoon that featured real gondolas and gondoliers imported from Italy, and a two-block business district noted for its covered arched walkways and Venetian Renaissance architecture. Aside from shops, restaurants, and hotels, Venice boasted the Abbott Kinney amusement park pier, home to numerous attractions including a 3,000-seat auditorium, a dance pavilion, and a large aquarium. Residents from outlying areas packed the Green Line interurban trolley cars so they could spend a day at the beach swimming, dancing, and riding the popular rides. A two-and-a-half-mile miniature railway also circled the town.

210 *(upper left)* and 208 Horizon Avenue *(upper right)* are relatively unchanged from how they appear in the 1914 movie.

This 1918 aerial view of Venice looks west towards the beach. The rectangle marks the location of the Race Thru the Clouds twin racing coaster that was demolished in 1924, the small ellipse marks the tall chimney of the Abbott Kinney Company Pump House (used to circulate fresh ocean water to the canals), and the large ellipse marks the corner of Second (now Main) and Westminster appearing in the film. Within the large ellipse we see the "T" intersection of Westminster, running west towards the ocean, and Second Avenue, terminating at Westminster at an oblique angle. Continuing south, the path of Second Avenue turns into the Coral Canal leading towards the lagoon further south.

These views of Chaplin were filmed looking south from the terminus of Second Avenue. The crowds and the gravity ramp block the view of the Coral Canal leading south towards the Venice lagoon. The Race Thru the Clouds racing coaster appears in the background (*rectangle*).

The tall chimney of the Abbott Kinney Company Pump House (*ellipse*), situated at 1502 Park Row off of Windward, appears in the background.

The movie frames *(left)* both look north up Second (now Main) from the same corner of Westminster featured earlier. The gabled-roof building to the left background of the top movie frame still stands at the southwest corner of Brooks Avenue and Second (Main) *(inset, upper right)*. The rectangle in each movie frame marks the extant building *(inset, lower right)* standing at the northeast corner of Breeze Avenue and Second (Main). The arrow marks the large natural gas storage tank mentioned on the next page.

Frustrated by Charlie's camera-hogging, the director character (played by Henry Lehrman) knocks Charlie to the ground *(inset, above)*. Lehrman, who directed Chaplin's first four films, including *Kid Auto*, is remembered for being engaged to actress Virginia Rappé. Her scandalous death following a 1921 Labor Day party hosted by film comedian Roscoe "Fatty" Arbuckle lead to Roscoe's trial for manslaughter by a politically ambitious district attorney. Lehrman served as the main prosecution witness. Though fully exonerated, Roscoe was banned by the Hays Commission from appearing in films for more than a decade.

This view was taken from atop the Race Thru the Clouds roller coaster, looking north across the lagoon up the Coral Canal. The ellipse marks the filming location at the corner of Second and Westminster. The left arrow shows the chimney of the Abbott Kinney pumping plant discussed previously, and the right arrow marks the gas storage tank mentioned on the prior page. The canal and lagoon were later filled in and paved over. The Antler Hotel building to the right, sporting the Venice News billboard, is still standing.

For the first time recorded on film, Chaplin executes his signature flick kick to a discarded cigarette butt *(left)*. The scene was also filmed looking north up Second (now Main) from the corner of Westminster. The same view today appears at the lower right.

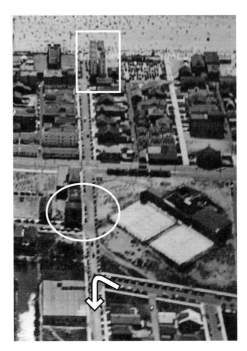

Charlie pauses in front of a group of bemused spectators. The center youth watching the auto race has "FIAT" emblazoned on his sweater, perhaps a precursor to the corporate brand affinity so prevalent today. Gerald Smith first identified this spot.

This view looks west down Westminster from the corner of Second (Main). The Ames Apartment appears in the background of both shots.

This aerial view, looking west, shows the Ames Apartment (ellipse) in relation to the corner of Second (Main) and Westminster (arrow). The country club tennis courts appear across the street. The far rectangle is the Waldorf Hotel, where Chaplin filmed scenes from *By the Sea*.

Charlie gazes at the camera. This view looks west down Westminster past the corner of Second. The arrow marks the direction of the race cars rounding the corner (inset). The crowd on the hill is watching from the tennis courts of the Southern California Writers Association's country club.

The once sparsely landscaped country club is now a popular dog park. The same view looking west today.

Chaplin's first close-up image recorded on film shows him scowling at a movie camera, a portent, perhaps, of the complicated relationship he would have with the fame and publicity resulting from being the world's first superstar. At the time, he was only 24.

The Race Thru the Clouds also appears in Buster Keaton's 1920 short film, *The High Sign*. Whereas Chaplin filmed looking south at the coaster, this shot was filmed looking east down what is now 18th Avenue.

Looking southeast at the north entrance of the Race Thru the Clouds.

Abject in romantic defeat, Harold Lloyd rides the Venice miniature railway into the sunset in this concluding shot from his 1920 short *Number Please?* The famous roller coaster, and the Race Thru the Clouds soda fountain, appear in the background.

Chaplin's first movie was filmed from January 5–9, 1914, his first week employed at the Keystone Studio. Charlie plays a con man who charms the fiancée of a newspaper reporter. After witnessing a spectacular auto accident, captured on film by the reporter, Charlie steals the reporter's camera and applies for work at the newspaper, submitting the stolen photographs as his own. The reporter chases Charlie around town, ending with a fight on the prow of a streetcar.

Chaplin filmed scenes *(below)* on the Broadway side of the former *Los Angeles Times* newspaper building, situated on the northeast corner of Broadway and First Street. This vintage view *(right)* was taken sometime after the Hall of Justice, which is still standing *(visible at the far left)* was completed in 1925.

Charlie contemplates his next move beside the Times building.

This detail matches where Chaplin stood.

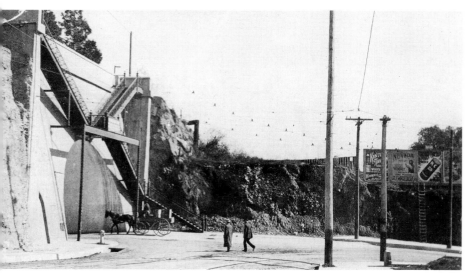

Los Angeles originally had several tunnels passing through hills that no longer exist. This view shows the south end of the Broadway Tunnel that ran for a short block from north of Temple to south of what is now Cesar Chavez Avenue. It was demolished long ago.

This frame shows Charlie running south down Broadway from First Street. The mouth of the Broadway Tunnel (ellipse) appears in the far distance, the Times building corner (square) appears to the right.

This view shows the block of Broadway appearing behind Chaplin during the scene below (lower arrow), starting at the Times building in the foreground, the distinctive Hall of Records behind it, with its variety of window shapes, and the mouth of the Broadway Tunnel at the end of the block. The top arrow marks the Court Flight funicular railway discussed in the Work chapter. A second section of tunnel along Hill Street (rectangle) continues under Fort Moore Hill.

View up Broadway from First. Today the tunnel and the old Hall of Records are gone, and the Times building site is now a parking garage.

Charlie runs around the corner, heading from east on First Street to south on Broadway.

This vintage view looks north up Broadway from the former city hall, located at 226 South Broadway, towards Charlie's position *(star)* near First and Broadway. The city hall pictured was built in 1889, and demolished after the current city hall opened in 1928.

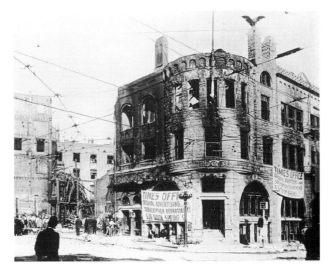

The bombed ruins of the Los Angeles Times Building.

Early on October 1, 1910, during a bitter labor dispute, a ferocious bomb explosion rocked the Los Angeles Times Building. Gigantic tanks of printing ink ignited, quickly spreading flames and killing at least 20. The fiercely anti-union owner-publisher of the *Times*, Civil War general Harrison Gray Otis, hired private detectives to scour the country for culprits. Hundreds of activists were rounded up nationwide, and labor leader brothers James and John McNamara were finally charged with the bombing. Famed trial lawyer Clarence Darrow was hired for the defense, convincing the brothers to plea bargain to avoid the death penalty. James received life; John 15 years for conspiracy. The guilty pleas shocked the public, and in a special run-off election pro-business incumbent mayor George Alexander defeated socialist/labor candidate Job Harriman, quelling the nascent Los Angeles labor movement for decades.

The *Times* operated from cramped auxiliary headquarters until the newly rebuilt Times building reopened on the same spot two years to the day of the bombing. Fifteen months later, Chaplin filmed at this same spot. The *Times* moved to its fourth and current headquarters at 123 S. Spring Street in 1935.

Charlie and the reporter, played by the film's director Henry Lehrman, fight it out at the corner of Fourth and Grand *(left)*. Behind Chaplin you can see a vertical sign for the Fremont Hotel at Fourth and Olive *(lower right)*. This vintage shot *(upper right)* shows nearly the same view. The Continental Building *(ellipse)*, completed in 1904, was the city's first skyscraper, standing at 174 feet. Because a 150-foot height restriction was imposed from 1905 until 1957, for decades the Continental remained the tallest building in downtown (excepting the modern city hall completed in 1928). The arrow in the movie frame and in the hotel photo are both pointing east down Fourth Street.

The spot today is surrounded to the north and south by towering skyscrapers. Looking east down Fourth Street, we can still see the Continental Building at the corner of Fourth and Spring Streets.

Chaplin's fourth film was shot after a torrential rainstorm soaked Los Angeles, explaining both the title and the sequences in the film where Charlie and Ford Sterling attempt to help Emma Clifton across a large curbside puddle. The many park sequences must have been filmed at either Lafayette Park or MacArthur (then Westlake) Park, both just a few blocks east of Shatto Place.

This aerial photo above Wilshire Boulevard was taken between 1923 and 1928. It shows from left to right the Ambassador Hotel (*square*), the Gaylord Apartments (named for eccentric developer and socialist Gaylord Wilshire) directly across the street from the Ambassador, the Talmadge Apartments (*rectangle*) built in 1923, and the corner of Shatto Place and Wilshire (*circle*). The Immanuel Presbyterian Church, standing due west of the Talmadge, would be built in 1928 some time after this photo was taken.

Charlie enjoys his rival's misfortunes. Behind him lies the northwest corner of Wilshire and Shatto Place, the visible section of the house facing Wilshire. A beautiful pergola flanking the house on the left can also be seen. Although not clear in this frame, the words "Shatto Place" are chiseled into the stone post. The home was built by Morris and Gusta Kornblum in 1910 at a cost exceeding $30,000. If newspaper accounts are to be believed, railroad baron Charles H. Sharp from Kansas City first visited the home the morning of March 9, 1911, purchased the home for $100,000 cash at noon the same day, and moved in with his wife that very evening, acquiring the mansion as a winter home. Actor Hobart Bosworth reportedly lived here during the 1930s.

This detail from the aerial photo shows that Chaplin returned a few blocks from his old haunts to film a scene from *City Lights (lower right)* nearly 17 years later. As Charlie and the drunk millionaire from that movie turn south off of Wilshire onto Berendo *(arrow)*, we see a multi-arched building on the corner, and the Gaylord Apartments further down the street.

Today the corner of Wilshire and Shatto Place has been subsumed by this new construction and the modern day Wilshire/Vermont Metro line station located at 3191 Wilshire Boulevard.

This shot from *City Lights* looks west down Wilshire towards the Gaylord Apartments.

Charlie's two favorite pastimes involve drinking in saloons and flirting with pretty girls. Roscoe "Fatty" Arbuckle plays one woman's outraged husband.

Many street scenes were filmed looking northeast up Flower Street from the corner of West Pico Boulevard. I first noticed that trolley cars ran along both streets of this intersection during the scene, and that there appeared to be a church a half-block up the street. Based on the shadows, I also concluded the view showed a northwest corner. By checking vintage maps *(inset)*, I found that Flower and Pico had intersecting trolley lines, located near the Christ Episcopal Church *(inset)*. After searching for Flower and Pico at the Los Angeles Public Library online photo collection, I quickly found this 1920s-era photo *(below right)* matching the exact spot.

The corner building was at one time the Hotel Watson, and later home to Fisk Tires on the ground floor. The Thomas Restaurant to the left advertises on its front window "all women cooks and bakers." Located near the Staples Center, today *(lower left)* the area has been wiped clean. Nothing remains, although today the Metro Blue Line light rail runs up Flower, mirroring its trolley line predecessor.

C harlie plays a waiter in a dive cabaret who rescues socialite Mabel Normand during a robbery. Mistaking him for a fellow blue blood, she invites him to her swank garden party. After Charlie returns to work from the party, a rival suitor who knows Charlie's true status suggests that the swells all go "slumming." Arriving at Charlie's cabaret, Mabel discovers his secret and rejects his appeals.

Most of the movie was filmed in the heart of Chinatown on Apablasa Street *(rectangle)*, east of and perpendicular to Alameda Street, running horizontally (north-south) across this vintage aerial photo of the plaza *(right)*. This circa-1980s photo of the plaza *(lower right)* shows how the Union Train Station east of Alameda has completely replaced the former setting.

In 1870, less than 200 of the 6,000 residents of Los Angeles were Chinese. Their numbers swelled as thousands were hired to help build the Southern Pacific Railroad connecting San Francisco and Los Angeles. Chinatown originated south of the Plaza de Los Angeles along Calle de Los Negros (Negro Alley) in the 1870s, and in the 1880s expanded east of the plaza on former grazing lands and vineyards owned by Mexican land baron Juan Apablasa and his son, Cayetano. Three Chinatown streets bear their names.

Crammed in among noisy and smoke-choked railroad tracks, a towering gasworks plant, and the often overflowing Los Angeles River, Chinatown was the city's least desirable address. Working mostly in laundries and as vegetable truck farmers, the Chinese endured discriminatory laws and taxes, and were denied property ownership.

The Chinese Exclusion Act of 1882 stopped further immigration, and prohibited resident laborers from bringing over their wives and children. The privately owned streets of Chinatown were never paved, and as lessees the Chinese suffered the neglect imposed by their landlords. Once the original leases expired, most of Chinatown was sold in 1914 to make way for the future Union Train Station. After years of litigation, the Chinese were evicted in 1934 for construction of the terminal which opened to great acclaim on May 7, 1939. In 1937, community leaders formulated a master plan to develop a new Chinatown between Hill and Broadway, a mile northwest from its former site, where it remains today.

Charlie sets off for work. He is standing at 311 Apablasa near the end of the first block of the street. Cayetano Alley *(square)* appears one block further east. Because Chinatown was photographed extensively before it was demolished, I was able to find these and other Chinatown locations simply by studying old photographs for clues.

This matching photo shows the north side of the 313–329 block of Apablasa. The rectangle marks the corner of Cayetano Alley visible in the Chaplin frame. The first building to the left, around the corner from where Chaplin stood, was the headquarters for the Chee Kung Tong, a Chinese secret association. Also known as the Bing Kong Tong, its major rival was the Hop Sing Tong headquartered in the Lugo Adobe discussed in *Easy Street*. During one so-called tong war, the Hop Sing murdered the two owners of a tailor shop at 323 Apablasa *(arrow)*. A few years later, in 1922, the police raided an underground den at this same address, finding "a veritable opium smokers' paradise," equipped with eight bunks and full paraphernalia. The police also found a cache of narcotics sewed in the lining of the proprietress's clothes.

Taken from the Alameda Street entrance to Chinatown, this view east shows the first block of Apablasa. The ellipse marks where Chaplin stood in the frame above.

This 1930s aerial view looks north at Apablasa running east from Alameda. The left arrow marks where Chaplin stood in the frame *(upper left)*, and the right arrow marks the corner of Cayetano Alley.

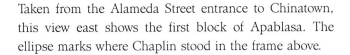

Standing under a porch, Charlie greets a woman in front of the "cabaret." They are standing around the corner from the prior shot *(below)*. Notice the bystanders watching in the background. A friend, Stephen Loo, translated the sign in the background as "*Yi De Shen.*" The last word, *Shen*, means "Victory," a common retail store name. The first two words (*Yi De*) could be the owner's name. But together the three words mean "Easy Victory." Since the Sanborn fire insurance maps identify this spot and the others beside it as gambling halls, perhaps Easy Victory is the correct translation.

Looking west back at the first block of Apablasa, this building stood like an island in the middle of the street. The back of the building faced Alameda Street. The ellipse marks Chaplin's spot in the lower left frame. The arrow in each frame turns from east to north.

This earlier shot is around the corner from the above shot.

The same building appears in this shot from famed director D.W. Griffith's 1919 Chinatown melodrama *Broken Blossoms*, set in the Limehouse District of London and starring Lillian Gish. (The popular film was known in the trade as "Busted Buds"). Chaplin stood under this same porch, and around the corner to the left.

Adding this vintage photo of the south side of Apablasa to the Chaplin frame creates a panoramic view where a merchant can be seen hosing down the dusty street. Privately owned, the streets of Chinatown were never paved.

Charlie is led away by the police during this scene from *The Kid*, filmed at the corner of Cayetano Alley. Nos. 330 and 328 Apablasa, on the south side of the street, appear behind him.

This view looks west down Apablasa, from one block further down the street. The arrow points to where Chaplin stood under the porch, and matches the direction of the arrow *(above)*. The ellipse shows the corner of Cayetano Alley where Chaplin stood in *The Kid*. The star marks the Los Angeles Railway Substation building that powered

the electric trolley lines. It still stands on Los Angeles Street *(inset above)*, and can be seen in Buster Keaton's *The Goat* (*see* Easy Street *chapter*).

Looking west, this matching frame from *Broken Blossoms* shows the north side of the same block of Apablasa. The vertical arrow marks Cayetano Alley.

Looking east, the society swells arrive in town for their slumming party. We are now further down Apablasa, one block east of Cayetano Alley. The corner in the background is Juan Street. The arrow in each frame is oriented east down the street.

This matching view (*above*) shows the 400 block of Apablasa past the corner of Juan Street.

Looking back west down Apablasa from Juan Street, now two blocks away from the "cabaret" porch described earlier. The vertical arrow here and above marks the corner of Cayetano Alley that appears in *The Kid*, and the ellipse marks the spot where the slumming party parked their car. In 1931, the police raided another opium den from the storefront to the right of the vertical arrow by bringing an old battering ram facetiously named the "Key to Chinatown" out of retirement. Shaped like a log with handles, two detectives facing each other would swing the heavy iron ram between them until the pointed tip of the ram punched out the lockset of the door.

The Chin Woo building stood between Marchessault Street to the south, and Apablasa Street to the north, facing Juan Street. This view of the building shows the corner of Marchessault to the left, and Juan to the right. The society swells parked their car *(upper right)* beneath the covered awning on Apablasa Street in the far background. The curved arrow in each image turns from east on Apablasa to south on Juan.

The Juan (east) side of the Chin Woo building appears behind Jackie Coogan and Tom Wilson in this scene from *The Kid (left)*. The same side of the Chin Woo building appears in this scene from Chaplin's 1915 film, *Police (right)*.

This 1930s view looks west towards the plaza (*trees, upper left*) as Alameda runs from left to right across the photo. At the center we see down the length of Apablasa Street appearing in the film. The top frames belong to the "cabaret" building at the west end of Apablasa, set off like an island in the middle of the street. The society swells parked their car (*right frame*) near the corner of Juan. The large Chin Woo building stands near the center on Juan between Marchessault and Apablasa. The frames from *The Kid* and *Police (below)* show the Juan side of the Chin Woo building. The star highlights the Los Angeles Railway Substation building mentioned earlier, and still standing on Los Angeles Street.

Looking north up Avalon at the corner of D Street in Wilmington.

Charlie plays a jealous wife who catches "her" husband, played by Mack Swain, flirting with another woman at a harbor festival. This marked Chaplin's first of three female impersonations to be captured on film; the others being *The Masquerader* (1914) and *A Woman* (1915).

A Busy Day was filmed in Wilmington on April 11, 1914, during a four-hour parade celebrating the opening of the Los Angeles Harbor expansion, built to accommodate the increased trade that would come from the Panama Canal which opened four months later.. The corner in the background is the northeast corner of Canal and East 3rd Streets, now Avalon and D Streets. Newspaper accounts of the parade include a photograph taken from nearly the same vantage point as used here. Avalon Street leads south to the north end of Slip No. 5 of the Los Angeles Harbor, discussed in *Modern Times*.

Wilmington was founded in 1858 by Yankee businessman Phineas Banning, named after his birthplace in Delaware. During the Civil War, the Lincoln administration spent nearly $1 million creating a military base in Wilmington, the Drum Barracks, that is now a museum.

In the background *(upper right)* we see the St. John's Episcopal Church *(lower right)*, built in 1883. It was sometimes known as the church on stilts, after having been raised eight feet when dirt from the harbor dredging was used to fill the lowlands surrounding the church. The interior included a huge cross made out of brass taken from a German submarine during World War I, and an altar, donated by the Banning family, made from marble quarried from nearby Santa Catalina Island.

This sketch of the church was drawn by Charles Owens, staff artist for the *Los Angeles Times*, in 1939.

This view looks north up Canal (now Avalon) at the corner of E. 3rd (now D Street). St. John's Episcopal Church stands up from the corner. Train tracks cross Canal Street on a diagonal.

The same view of the northeast corner of Avalon and D Street today. The white lines approximate the former train tracks (left) visible in the vintage image.

One block further south, this 1930s-era view looks north up Avalon from C Street. The ellipse marks the St. John's Episcopal Church visible in the movie frame.

The corresponding view up Avalon from C Street today.

Mabel's Busy Day

Released June 13, 1914

Gentlemen of Nerve
Released October 29, 1914

Mabel's Busy Day finds Mabel Normand selling hot dogs at the auto racetrack. While other customers steal from her, Charlie makes off with her entire tray, and Mabel calls the police on him. *Gentlemen of Nerve* is also set at the auto racetrack, and features Charlie's antics as he sneaks in without an admission ticket and steals sips of soda from pretty girls sitting in the stands.

The Ascot Park Speedway was originally a horse racetrack. In both this frame from *Mabel (center)* and *Gentlemen (right)* you can see what was a saddling paddock where the horses were stabled. The ellipse matches the ellipse in the panoramic shot below, taken March 5, 1916, at the $50,000 100-mile Washington Sweepstakes. The event was so well-attended that the paddock roof is jammed with spectators *(inset)*.

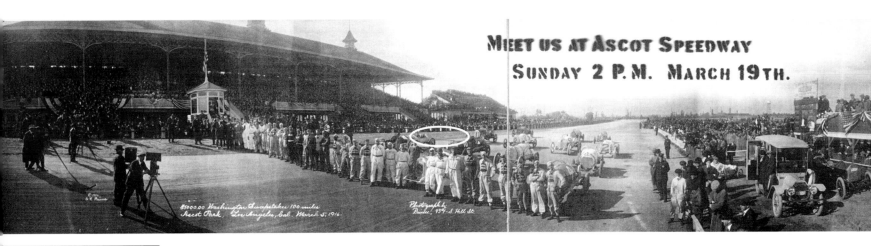

MEET US AT ASCOT SPEEDWAY
SUNDAY 2 P.M. MARCH 19TH.

The mile-long Ascot Park racecourse was built in 1903, situated on Slauson Avenue between South Park Avenue and South Central. The frame from *Mabel* (*right*) shows how dusty the racecourse was before they began spraying oil on the dirt track late in 1915. This improvement nearly doubled the racers' speed from 40 to 80 miles an hour. In 1916, the turns were further banked, and then paved with asphalt. "No Dust!" boasted the newspaper ads of the day.

Barney Oldfield, Eddie Pullen, and Teddy Tetzlaff were among the popular race car drivers of the time. Admission for a day's racing (parking included) was $1, perhaps 10 times or more the price of a movie ticket. Aside from the auto races, patrons would delight in aerial stunts performed by pilots such as Helen Klekar, Champion Lady Pilot of America, and Katherine Stinson, the international Champion Girl Flier.

This aerial view looking north shows the entire field.

This frame from *Gentlemen* shows the starting line, with the saddling paddock visible in the background.

This frame from *Gentlemen* shows the track leader board, appearing to the right in the panorama on the previous page.

Mabel's Married Life

Released June 20, 1914

Husband Charlie and wife Mabel Normand squabble after a brutish prizefighter (Mack Swain) flirts with Mabel in the park. Charlie seeks fortification at a saloon, then returns home so inebriated he mistakes Mabel's recently acquired boxing dummy as his rival.

Looking north, two couples quarrel on the island in the Echo Park Lake, its distinctive bridge appearing in the background. A bystander on the bridge can be seen observing the filming. Notice the gnarled, rustic bridge handrails.

Echo Park is located between Glendale Boulevard and Echo Park Avenue, roughly a mile northwest from downtown, and just five blocks south of the Keystone Studio. Echo Park started out in 1868 as Reservoir No. 4 of The Los Angeles Canal and Reservoir Co., storing water from the Los Angeles River with a dam to the south constructed along Belleview Avenue.

In the 1880s, carriage maker Thomas Kelley bought most of the land around the reservoir. In 1891, the city determined that the dam was not safe, and dramatically lowered the water level. The city struck a deal with Kelley, swapping property, so that land once submerged by the reservoir would be made into a park. Echo Park first opened in 1895, and is surrounded by historic homes, bungalows, and apartment buildings.

Echo Park has appeared frequently in the movies for nearly 90 years. In one notable appearance, when Mack Sennett learned that the lake would be drained for maintenance, his crew improvised a comedy on the spot, frolicking in the muddy lake bottom (1913's *A Muddy Romance*). Apparently, by 1918 the city leaders banned Keystone from filming at the park because too many flowers were being trampled.

This representative view of the park was taken circa 1920, after the rustic bridge handrails were replaced with smooth lumber.

In both the movie and in this circa-1900 image, the Echo Park Bridge handrails were constructed with irregular gnarled wood. This distinguishing feature appears in the films identified on the next page.

This image of Charlie by the Echo Park Bridge appears in *Twenty Minutes of Love* (1914).

Mabel's boat is stranded on the drained lake bottom in *A Muddy Romance*. The park bridge appears in the background.

This is the Echo Park Bridge as it appears today. At some point the bridge was rebuilt with steel, and now has a different cantilever design underneath. The bridge is closed, so it is no longer possible to visit the island where so many Keystone films were made.

Mabel Normand plays a scene beside the bridge in *Mabel's Dramatic Career* (1913).

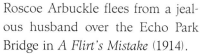

Roscoe Arbuckle flees from a jealous husband over the Echo Park Bridge in *A Flirt's Mistake* (1914).

Mack Sennett points out to Roscoe Arbuckle that Mack's girl, Mabel, is now appearing on the cinema screen in *Mabel's Dramatic Career*.

This USGS satellite photo shows the distinctive "thumb and mitten" north end of the Echo Park Lake, and its trademark island. Glendale Boulevard runs along the left, and Echo Park Avenue runs along the right.

Here Charlie appears on the bridge in *Recreation* (1914). Notice the gnarled handrails.

Laughing Gas

Released July 9, 1914

Charlie wreaks havoc as a flirtatious dental assistant who decides to treat the patients himself.

Charlie confronts Mack Swain outside the Sunset Pharmacy, located at 1572 West Sunset Boulevard, at the southeast corner of Echo Park Avenue. The store was only one short block north of Echo Park, where many Keystone comedies were filmed. This view looks south down Echo Park Avenue.

Looking north up Echo Park Avenue towards the corner of Sunset, the Sunset Pharmacy appears to the far right. This scene is from the 1925 Sennett film, *Good Morning, Nurse!* Ralph Graves is behind the wheel, while Marvin Loback stands to the side.

The same intersection of Sunset and Echo Park appears in this frame from Roscoe Arbuckle's *Mabel and Fatty's Married Life* (1915), only looking east down Sunset past Echo Park Avenue. The corner where Chaplin filmed is out of view to the right.

Brent Walker found this spot. Chaplin's former co-star, Ben Turpin, appears with Phyllis Haver across from the same corner in *Bright Eyes* (1921). The spot on the far corner where Chaplin stood is behind Phyllis's shoulder.

Today the pharmacy is a branch of Bank of America.

THE KEYSTONE FILM CO.
©1914 KESSEL & BAUMANN

As the newly hired office janitor, Charlie predictably makes a mess, and is fired. While leaving the premises, he catches a thief breaking into the company's safe, and rescues a secretary.

Washing windows, Charlie nearly falls out of the Marsh-Strong Building as four onlookers (*inset*) lean out to watch the filming. On the far corner is Tom Mack's Cafe, located at 858 S. Main Street, or 9th and Main. An auction notice reports that the cafe had a full-length mahogany bar, fine oil paintings, and chandeliers, yet also a 24-seat counter and ice cream tables.

The Tom Mack Cafe building still stands today at the northeast corner of 9th and Main.

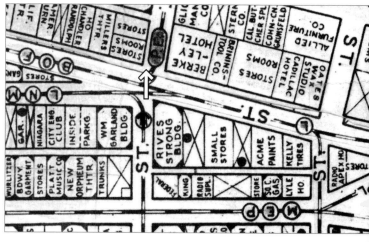

The arrow on this 1930s map pointing south down 9th matches the frame (*left*), where you can see the trolley tracks split off from Main Street onto Spring Street. Spring merges into Main before 9th, resulting in a narrow triangular intersection.

A contemporary view of the arched second-story windows on 9th Street, east of the Tom Mack Cafe site.

Looking north up Los Angeles Street, the back of the Marsh–Strong Building appears in the upper left corner of this frame from Keaton's 1922 short *Cops*, as Buster rides down the street south past 10th Street.

Charlie peered out from the Marsh–Strong Building (1913) standing at the southwest corner of 9th and Main. Based on the photo details, I estimate Charlie was six floors up and two windows down from the fire escape *(ellipse)* where the cameraman likely stood while filming the shot.

This vintage view north shows a "Y" intersection as Spring Street merges into the more prominent Main Street. The arrow points east down 9th from the Marsh–Strong Building towards the partially obscured Tom Mack Cafe building.

416-418 South Broadway

Charlie and Mack Swain play piano movers who carelessly switch orders, re-possessing a wealthy customer's piano while delivering another piano to a deadbeat. In this frame *(far right)* you can see the shop name of an actual piano store, Wiley B. Allen Co., located at 416–418 South Broadway. The shop window reflects the distinctive window pattern of the Grant Building across the street located on the northwest corner of Fourth and Broadway.

This vintage view looking north up Broadway almost includes the Allen Co. store at the far right edge. The pyramid-capped tower up the street was Los Angeles City Hall at the time, located at 226 S. Broadway. Completed in 1889, it was demolished in 1928 after the current city hall opened that same year.

The former Los Angeles City Hall.

The setting today is home to many small markets.

How time does change.

The Grant Building, built in 1902 on the corner of Fourth and Broadway, was originally seven stories high. It has since been cut down to two floors, and is now home to a
noodle shop. The office building located at 353 S. Broadway, due north of the Grant
Building, was built in 1913. It has been striped of all ornamentation, and its windows
are covered over for use as a storage warehouse. The building hosts a dramatic mural
(*inset*), *Calle de la Eternidad* (1993), by Johanna Poethig, sponsored as part of the Social
and Public Art Resources Center (SPARC) program.

I n this "park" comedy, Charlie and Mack Swain inadvertently switch overcoats after quarreling in a cafe. Chaos ensues when their wives find incriminating notes in their switched garments. Here, actress Phyllis Allen frets over a note she thinks belongs to her husband. A small portion of the Hollenbeck Park Bridge appears in the background. This poor quality image *(inset)* reveals a longer section of the bridge.

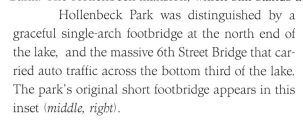

Boating at Hollenbeck Park, Los Angeles, Cal.

This movie was likely filmed in Hollenbeck Park, situated between East 4th Street and Wilshire (then East 6th Street), just east of the Golden State Freeway (5) in Boyle Heights, an early Los Angeles suburb located east of the Los Angeles River. Opening in 1892, the long and narrow park runs north-south, surrounding a man-made lake. The park was built on land donated by Mayor William Workman, and was named in honor of Workman's friend, John E. Hollenbeck, founder of the First National Bank. The Hollenbeck mansion, which still stands across from the park, is now a home for the aged.

Hollenbeck Park was distinguished by a graceful single-arch footbridge at the north end of the lake, and the massive 6th Street Bridge that carried auto traffic across the bottom third of the lake. The park's original short footbridge appears in this inset *(middle, right)*.

Hollenbeck Park appears in Harold Lloyd's 1924 feature, *Girl Shy (left)*, and is shown when he attempts suicide *(right)* in his 1920 short film *Haunted Spooks*. This bridge also appears in the Laurel and Hardy short film *Men O'War* (1929), and likely in many other films.

The Hollenbeck Park stone pergola appears in this scene *(left)* from Roscoe Arbuckle's 1915 short film, *Fatty's Chance Acquaintance*. It can also be seen in this shot *(right)* from *Fatty's Tintype Tangle* (1915).

I know from studying vintage photos and newspaper accounts that Hollenbeck Park's original short footbridge *(middle inset, prior page)* stood north of the park boathouse, while a taller footbridge similar in appearance was built south of the boathouse, probably in 1915. Because the bridge appearing behind Phyllis Allen in the 1914 frame appears to be lower to the water than the bridge in the 1924 *Girl Shy* frame, my sense is that Chaplin filmed the original low bridge, before the taller bridge was built. I know conclusively that *Girl Shy* was filmed at Hollenbeck Park, as the 6th Street Bridge, the arched footbridge, and the park pergola all appear in the film.

This vintage view looking north from the former 6th Street Bridge shows the arched footbridge in the far background and the stone pergola appearing in the scenes above.

The arched footbridge and the 6th Street Bridge were removed long ago. Only a small remnant of the stone pergola stands by the lake today.

Released at a time when even feature-length dramas were still a novelty, this landmark film is widely recognized as America's first feature-length comedy. Broadway star Marie Dressler reprised her stage role as Tillie, a naïve farm girl who succumbs to an urban con man, played here by Chaplin.

After a mishap with the "big city" traffic and trolleys *(right)*, Marie helps Charlie to his feet. Brent Walker discovered this spot by looking up "Wright Hardware," barely visible to the left, in an old city directory. The arrow marks 6410–6146 Hollywood Boulevard in each image.

Although the corner building added another floor, and underwent an art deco remodeling, perhaps in 1926, the adjoining building, with its stepped façade and horizontal roofline elements, appears relatively unchanged.

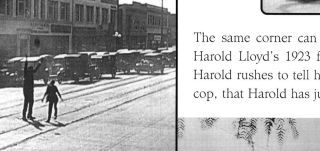

The same corner can be seen at the end of Harold Lloyd's 1923 feature, *Why Worry?*, as Harold rushes to tell his friend, a giant traffic cop, that Harold has just become a father.

This view shows the southwest corner of Cahuenga and Hollywood Boulevard. The trolley line on Hollywood Boulevard appears in the movie. The Hollywood National Bank stood on the corner, followed by a barbershop (notice the barber pole), the Wright Hardware store, a grocery store, and another hardware store.

In this famous shot from Buster Keaton's 1922 short film, *Cops*, Buster escapes a mob of police by grabbing the back of a passing car with one hand, getting whisked out of frame in the process. In the far background, we see the Palmer Building—the future home of the now defunct *Hollywood Daily Citizen* newspaper—under construction.

Standing at the bank corner, Charlie and Mabel conspire to relieve Tillie of her fortune. A barber pole and a hardware store sign (at 6402 and 6414 respectively) are shown in the background. I am intrigued by the woman seen leaving the bank. Her Victorian-era full-length skirt and high-collared blouse would soon give way to the flapper fashions of the Roaring Twenties.

On the opposing corner from where Chaplin had filmed *Tillie* 22 years earlier, the Security Bank building, still standing at the northeast corner of Hollywood and Cahuenga *(see aerial photo, right)*, appears briefly in

this scene from *Modern Times*, as Charlie welcomes Paulette Goddard into a police paddy wagon.

The mouth of the alley appearing in *Cops (oval)* is situated on Cahuenga just below the southeast corner of Hollywood Boulevard. The corner where Chaplin filmed *Tillie* eight years earlier *(box)* was located just across the street. The six-story Security Bank building stands on the northeast corner.

Standing on the porch of the Hollywood Hotel, Mabel prepares herself for a confrontation with Charlie. Situated on the northwest corner of Hollywood and Highland, the Hollywood Hotel *(right)* was one of Hollywood's most prominent landmarks. It was built in 1903, and by 1914 had become the center of Hollywood life.

The porch of the hotel also appears in this scene from the 1919 Fay Tincher short film, *Rowdy Ann*.

The low railing, striped awnings and curtains, bay windows, porch columns, and rocking chairs that appear in the movie frame *(upper left)* also show up in this enlarged view *(left)* of the hotel porch.

Demolished in 1956, the site of the Hollywood Hotel is now home to the Hollywood & Highland Retail and Entertainment Center, known for its towering Babylon Court shopping mall patterned after the set from D.W. Griffith's 1916 masterpiece, *Intolerance*. The site is adjacent to the Kodak Theatre (2001), home to the annual Academy Awards ceremonies, and Grauman's Chinese Theatre (1927).

This view shows the Keystone Studio main gate and entrance door on Allesandro Street.

Two cops bring an inebriated Marie (Tillie) into the police station for questioning. Notice the word "POLICE" painted on the sidewalk. Comparing the identical door and window features with the photo (left), this scene must have been filmed in front of the Keystone Studio entrance door.

Taken from a hilltop, this view looks east towards the front of the Keystone Studio along Allesandro (Glendale) Street. The entrance door appears to the right of the open studio gate. The homes to the left pictured on Aaron Street are still standing, as is the large shooting stage on Effie Street in the right background. The long, two-story building to the right of the entrance door housed the studio dressing rooms.

In this frame from *Fatty's Plucky Pup* (1915), Fatty Arbuckle rides a bicycle north up Allesandro, from the corner of Effie, towards the same studio door, where the word "POLICE" can still be seen painted on the sidewalk. A prop Police Station sign has been added to the wall for effect.

Incorrectly assuming she has inherited her uncle's fabulous estate, Charlie and Marie celebrate their quickie marriage *(below)* in front of the gates of the Castle Sans Souci *(right)*, owned by Dr. A.G.R. Schloesser, formerly located in Hollywood at 1901 Argyle, above Franklin.

Once a practicing physician, Dr. Schloesser made his fortune in mining and real estate investments, becoming a prominent Hollywood booster, capitalist, and art connoisseur. Dr. Schloesser made several world tours, collecting a gallery of medieval paintings, tapestries, and statuary. Designed by architects Dennis & Farwell, the castle incorporated elements from ancient structures at Oxford, the Castle Glengarry in Scotland, and the Neurenberg Castle in Germany. Set in the foothills on a former lemon grove, the castle commanded a breathtaking view of Hollywood, especially from its six-story tower.

The castle doorway was an exact copy of the entrance to the city hall in Bremen, Germany, while the entrance was guarded by two Carrara marble lions bought at auction in Italy, which stood guard over the Palace of the Doges in Venice for nearly 150 years before being shipped to Hollywood. The baronial entrance hall measured 50 x 25 feet, and was finished in oak, with a heavily beamed ceiling 25 feet above the floor, a massive stone fireplace, and a row of niches housing suits of armor. The elaborate grounds were designed by Nils Emitslof, the former landscape artist for the Czar of Russia.

Before building Castle Sans Souci in 1912, Dr. Schloesser had built a similarly styled castle home four years earlier across the street at 1904 Argyle, known locally as Castle Glengarry. Dr. Schloesser sold Castle Glengarry in 1912 to a prominent New York banker for $100,000. Responding to anti-German sentiments during the First World War, Dr. Schloesser legally changed his name to Dr. Castles, a fitting self-tribute to the creator of two of Hollywood's greatest lost landmarks.

Charlie and Marie in front of the Castle Sans Souci gate.

Charlie and Marie revel at the prospect of living in such a grand estate.

The unidentified dapper gentleman posing with Mabel Normand and Marie Dressler is most likely Dr. Schloesser himself. His pose and attire appear identical to that of the gentleman posing in the postcard photo of the Schloesser mansion *(right)*. For perspective the same marble lion *(oval)* is marked in the postcard and movie frames.

MARIE DRESSLER
IN
"TILLIE'S PUNCTURED ROMANCE"

The Ocean Park Bathhouse was built in 1905 along Ocean Front between Navy and Ozone Avenues, near the foot of the Ocean Park Pier.

Once Charlie and Mabel's larcenous scheme is revealed, Marie grabs a revolver and chases them along pier settings Chaplin used previously in *His New Profession* (1914). Here Charlie swoons as Mabel tries to steady him. This scene was filmed at the Abbott-Kinney Pier in Venice, the most prominent amusement pier at the time, where Chaplin returned to film scenes from *By The Sea* and *The Adventurer*. Above Charlie's outstretched hand you can make out the distinctive minarets and domed roof of the Ocean Park Bathhouse. Since the shore is to the right (*east*), this view must be looking north. The Abbott Kinney Pier was the only pier situated south of the Ocean Park Bathhouse from which this view could be achieved.

This vintage view was taken from the Abbott Kinney Pier looking north along the beachfront, with the Ocean Park Bathhouse and Ocean View Hotel visible to the far left.

The bathhouse has long since been demolished, but the adjacent Ocean View Hotel, built in 1912 at the northeast corner of Ocean Front and Rose Avenue, still stands today.

The Essanay Studio

In 1907, film distributor George K. Spoor ("S") and actor/filmmaker Gilbert M. Anderson ("A") combined their talents and initials ("S" and "A") to form the Essanay Film Manufacturing Company in Chicago. Anderson would soon become famous for his characterization of Broncho Billy, the world's first cowboy movie star. While Spoor remained in Chicago at the primary studio, Anderson sought authentic locations for his films, and after working in various locations throughout California and the West, established a second Essanay unit in Niles, California, in 1912. Originally housed in a barn, Anderson constructed the Niles Studio in 1913 at the southwest corner of Front Street (now Niles Boulevard) and G Street.

During his brief tenure with Keystone in 1914, Chaplin had risen from obscurity to become an international celebrity. When his one-year Keystone contract was due to expire, Chaplin demanded that his $150 weekly salary be raised to $1,000. Sennett balked, complaining that this exceeded even his own salary. Anderson seized the opportunity, and signed Chaplin with Essanay in November 1914 at a weekly salary of $1,250. During 1915, Chaplin would make 14 short films for Essanay, filming in Chicago, Niles, San Francisco, Oakland, and Los Angeles.

Charlie applies for work as a propertyman at the "Lockstone" movie studio, a playful dig at Chaplin's former employer. When the leading man fails to appear for his scene in a historical drama, Charlie is called to take his place before the camera, disrupting the production.

Chaplin's first film for the Essanay Studio was appropriately titled *His New Job*. Chaplin visited the Essanay studio in Niles for the first time in mid-December 1914, and was unimpressed both with the facility and its remote location, an hour southeast from San Francisco. Chaplin decided to begin his contract at the main Essanay studio in Chicago instead, and arrived in town shortly before Christmas. G.M. Anderson had hired Chaplin at $1,250 per week, and promised him a $10,000 signing bonus. Remarkably, Anderson's partner George Spoor was unaware of the Chaplin phenomenon sweeping the planet, and was outraged at Chaplin's prohibitive cost at a time when other Essanay stars pulled in only $75 per week. Spoor deliberately snubbed Chaplin on his arrival, and put off paying Chaplin's promised bonus for weeks.

Work on the film began in January 1915, and was released on February 1. By the time Spoor realized what a valuable property he had acquired, it was too late. Displeased with his ill treatment, Essanay's regimented production methods, and the harsh Chicago winter, Chaplin decided to fulfill the balance of his contract back in California.

Chaplin was paired with vaudeville veteran Ben Turpin, whose trademark crossed-eyes were jokingly insured for a million dollars if they should ever became uncrossed. Turpin, and fellow Essanay comedian Leo White, would join Chaplin in California to work on Charlie's next film.

The row homes on the north side of Chicago's W. Argyle Street appear through an open studio door.

Future silent screen legend Gloria Swanson, an unknown actress at the time, appeared as a typist behind Chaplin and Turpin in this scene (notice the Lockstone name painted on the glass door). Gloria later moved to Hollywood where she starred in a number of Mack Sennett Keystone comedies before becoming an acclaimed dramatic actress in the 1920s. Today, she may be best known for playing reclusive silent film star Norma Desmond in Billy Wilder's 1950 noir classic, *Sunset Boulevard*.

The Essanay Film Manufacturing Company was established in 1907 at 501 N. Wells Street in Chicago. Its first release, *An Awful Skate, or the Hobo on Rollers,* showed Ben Turpin skating into pedestrians on the studio front sidewalk. In 1909, the company moved to much larger studios located at 1333 W. Argyle Street on Chicago's north side, building an addition in 1914, and a further addition at 1345 W. Argyle in 1916. When Chaplin's contract ended in 1916, the Essanay Studio quickly fell on hard times, and closed forever in 1918.

Spoor sold the Chicago studio to former employees Donald Bell and Albert Howell for use by their namesake motion picture camera and equipment company, Bell & Howell. In 1973, the Bell & Howell corporation donated the Essanay buildings to a local public television station, and after passing through several hands, they now comprise part of the St. Augustine College campus. Though heavily remodeled, remnants of the studio still remain, including the stage where Chaplin filmed, now called the Charlie Chaplin Auditorium. The Essanay buildings were designated as Chicago historical landmarks in 1996.

This entrance to the 1916 studio addition still bears the Essanay studio name and Indian Chief head logo.

This vintage view shows mostly the 1916 addition to the Essanay Studio on 1345 W. Argyle. The Chaplin stage is a bit off camera to the left.

This modern view looks east down the 1916 addition of the studio towards the white portal entrance extending towards the sidewalk. The Chaplin stage lies past the portal door further down the street.

Following the filming of *His New Job* in Chicago, *A Night Out* was the first of five Essanay films Chaplin shot at the Niles studio in Northern California. Charlie is teamed once again with Ben Turpin, playing a pair of drunken ne'er-do-wells. Nineteen-year-old Edna Purviance makes her screen debut as the lovely married woman residing across the hall from Charlie's hotel room. From this point onward (with the exception of Chaplin's solo comedy, *One A.M.*), Edna would appear in every film Chaplin made until his 1925 masterpiece, *The Gold Rush*.

David Kiehn, author of the wonderful account of the Essanay Studio, *Broncho Billy and the Essanay Film Company*, and historian for the Niles Essanay Silent Film Museum, found a humorous newspaper story that while filming at the Hotel Oakland in Oakland, California, Chaplin and Turpin played a scene so convincingly they were very nearly arrested for public intoxication. The Hotel Oakland still stands between Harrison and Alice at 13th, but whatever scenes were filmed there do not seem to appear in the film. However, the Hotel Oakland clue led David to do a little sleuthing on foot, where he found nearby both the Peralta Apartments and the Sierra Apartments appearing in the movie.

Charlie nurses a bruise on the steps of the Sierra Apartments, located at 1502 Alice Street in Oakland, a half-block northeast of the Hotel Oakland.

The Sierra Apartments as it appears today.

This detail matches where Chaplin stood.

The same view today.

Charlie plans his next scheme in front of the Peralta Apartments at 184 13th Street in Oakland, one-and-a-half blocks southeast of the Hotel Oakland.

Ben Turpin and Charlie give actor Leo White a hard time. Gerald Smith noticed that the prop menu on the table *(insert)* came from the Hotel Wesley *(see next chapter)*, and was presumably stolen or borrowed by the property man from the hotel two blocks east of the Essanay Studio in Niles.

Downtrodden Charlie's fortunes change when he lands a job as the sparring partner for a local prizefighter. With a little luck, and the assistance of a horseshoe concealed in his glove, Charlie wins the day and the affection of Edna Purviance.

This view looking south shows the Essanay Studio located in Niles, California, at the southwest corner of Niles Boulevard and G Street. The photo was taken in December 1913, about a year before Chaplin first arrived in Niles before traveling to Chicago to begin his Essanay contract. The small bungalows hugging the studio buildings were built for the Essanay employees. Technically a district of Fremont, California, the community of Niles is situated about 35 miles southeast of San Francisco near the base of the East Bay foothills.

This view shows the Essanay Studio at Niles, perhaps in 1928. When Chaplin's contract came up for renewal in December 1915, Essanay was not able to retain him. The studio shut down on February 16, 1916, shortly after Chaplin completed his contract. Following vain attempts to resurrect the studio over the years, the studio building was finally demolished in July 1933. The rectangle marks the studio fence gate discussed in two pages.

During a requisite chase, Charlie runs past the corner of the Essanay Studio building.

Today the site is still a vacant lot.

Charlie saunters south down G Street towards Second Street along a distinctive board fence. The pitched roof of a studio bungalow *(square)* appears overhead.

The same view today, only the fence is now made of common chain-link.

The bungalows appearing in the movie, and in this vintage shot, were built for the studio employees. The bungalow on the northwest corner of G Street and Second Street was at one time occupied by Chaplin's longtime cameraman, Rollie Totheroh, while comedian Ben Turpin occupied a bungalow next door. Although Rollie was employed as a cameraman at the Niles Essanay Studio, he did not start working regularly with Chaplin until 1916, when Chaplin began his Mutual contract in Hollywood. (Totheroh may have filmed Chaplin's cameo appearance in Broncho Billy Anderson's *His Regeneration* (1915).) Their remarkable collaboration as artist and cameraman would last for nearly 40 years.

The same view today.

During a chase, Charlie runs east through the studio fence gate onto G Street. The two-story building in the background is the Niles Township Register *(inset)*, home of the local newspaper that was located on Niles Boulevard.

This reverse view of the G Street studio gate shows part of the glass atrium studio behind Charlie.

Looking west, this view shows the G Street side of the Essanay Studio. From left to right we see the bungalow and studio fence that appeared in the earlier frame, the large glass atrium studio, the open gate fence, and the main studio building.

Edna Purviance, Chaplin, and aviator Lincoln Beachey on the sidewalk in front of the Niles Essanay Studio *(left)*, taken January 29, 1915, shortly after Edna was first hired to become Chaplin's leading lady. Notice the billboards in the background that appear in the aerial shot of the studio.

After finishing *His New Job* at the Chicago Essanay Studio on January 12, Chaplin fled the harsh winter and hostile working conditions, and returned to Niles on January 18, taking comic actors Ben Turpin and Leo White along with him. Author David Kiehn reports that upon his arrival, Chaplin was dissatisfied with the potential leading ladies already working at the Niles studio. As a result, the company ran an ad the next day in the *San Francisco Chronicle*: "WANTED—THE PRETTIEST GIRL IN CALIFORNIA to take part in a moving picture." In response to the ad, three aspiring actresses, including Edna Purviance, arrived in town, registering at the Niles Belvoir Hotel on January 21. Presumably she and Chaplin met the next day.

Chaplin was initially hesitant to hire Edna, but her beauty and sense of humor balanced well with Charlie's antics, and the couple soon fell in love. Chaplin biographer David Robinson quotes from extant love notes that Chaplin and Edna exchanged on March 1, 1915 during the production of *The Champion*. Chaplin tells Edna she is the cause of him being "the happiest person in the whole world" and she responds that "nobody else in the world ... could have given me so much joy." Edna would appear in all of Chaplin's films for the next seven years, even following Chaplin's shotgun marriage to Mildred Harris in 1918. Although Edna retired from filmmaking in 1926, she would remain on the Chaplin Studio payroll until it closed in 1952, when Chaplin was denied reentry into America, and relocated to Switzerland.

Charlie trains for the big fight by jogging in the open studio yard. Notice the distinctive fence running along G Street in the background

The same view today. The rectangle marks matching profiles of a nearby ridgeline. The top of the Edison Theater, discussed in a few pages, appears within the box on the movie frame *(left)*.

This view shows the gymnasium set. In the far left background you can see stacks of film canisters.

This view shows part of the gymnasium set constructed within the large glass atrium studio. A close-up view of the set appears to the right. The heavyset man with his back to the camera (*arrow*) may be Roscoe Arbuckle stopping by to visit.

This view shows the larger atrium studio looking in the other direction. Some of the employee bungalows appear in the background.

Here's how the set appears in the film.

After more than an 80-year gap, the Edison Theater has been restored to its original purpose, and is home to the Niles Essanay Silent Film Museum. (www.nilesfilmmuseum.org)

Run by David Kiehn, Dorothy Bradley, and other dedicated film historians and local volunteers, the museum hosts Saturday night screenings of classic silent films, as well as the popular weekend-long Broncho Billy Silent Film Festival each June that attracts visitors from across the country. I find it altogether remarkable that Chaplin's films continue to be enjoyed 90 years later at the very spot where they were filmed, and within the very theater where Chaplin and his crew first watched them.

This shot shows Edna, Charlie, and out-of-town visitors in front of a small house. The large building in the background was the Edison Theater, a small movie theater located at 37417 Niles Boulevard, a half-block east from the Essanay Studio (barely visible in the far background) *(square)*. The theater opened on November 4, 1913, and it was here that Chaplin and the rest of the Essanay cast and crew would come to watch movies. In 1923, a bigger theater was built next door on the far side, but it was destroyed by a fire in 1959.

Today, the beautiful hotel building is relatively unchanged.

This vintage view shows the Hotel Wesley two short blocks east of the studio. Chaplin may have stayed here after first arriving in town, and most certainly ate lunch here during breaks in shooting. A pilfered menu from this hotel appears as a prop in Chaplin's first Niles comedy, *A Night Out*.

The community of Niles is justifiably proud of its early filmmaking heritage. The lampposts along Niles Boulevard, the town's main drag, are decorated with celebratory artwork and banners. For an online tour of Niles and more Niles history visit www.niles.org.

This vintage sign proclaims Niles's movie heritage.

Visitors entering Niles from the east are greeted by this sign.

Niles Boulevard is lined with quaint antique shops and restaurants. A local bar displays this figure of Charlie by the front door.

A recent plaque honors Niles's past.

A Jitney Elopement

Released April 1, 1915

Charlie rescues Edna from an arranged marriage to a European count by posing as the intended beau neither she nor her father have met. When the real count arrives, he and Edna's father chase Charlie and Edna alongside San Francisco's Golden Gate Park and Ocean Beach until the men's car plunges into the bay at Fisherman's Wharf.

The count arrives at Edna's house *(right)*. Except for the upcoming wharf shot, Gerald Smith discovered all of the locations in this chapter. He spotted this setting, looking east down Beulah Street at Cole Avenue in the background, by first noticing it in an aerial photo. Most of San Francisco west of the downtown business district is laid out in an orderly grid of rectangular street blocks, with only a few "T" intersections. Although there has been some remodeling, the houses in the background along Cole Avenue, and even the rooftops in the far background, all match the movie frame precisely. Further, none of the other "T" intersections in the area are even remotely similar to this setting. While some elements at the far right edge of the frame do not seem to match the setting today, there is no other likely candidate for this filming spot.

Looking down Beulah at Cole.

Charlie poses as the count.

This vintage photo matches the movie frame.

The authorities chase Charlie and Edna past the Murphy Windmill at the far southwest corner of Golden Gate Park, and beyond the stone arch bridge where Lincoln Way terminates at the Great Highway along the coast.

The Murphy Windmill is being restored. Built in 1905, it was the largest windmill in the world, and its 114-foot-long sails rotated clockwise, contrary to Dutch tradition. Together with the older Dutch Windmill located in the northwest corner of Golden Gate Park, the two windmills pumped water into an irrigation system that helped create the verdant park from an expanse of rolling sand dunes.

Charlie is determined to protect Edna from the count.

The same view today.

Continuing the chase, Charlie and Edna race north up the Great Highway towards Sutro Heights. The Pacific Ocean lies a few yards to the left.

The chase races past 1520–1522 Great Highway, between Kirkham Street and Lawton Street.

The same view today. Gerald Smith, with the help of other Chaplin fans, has developed a unique hobby of producing private "Then and Now" films that either re-create Chaplin's films at the original locations, or incorporate Chaplin settings into otherwise original stories. Many of the present-day frames in this chapter come from Gerald's films.

This aerial view looks east down the length of Golden Gate Park, with the Murphy Windmill and stone arch bridge appearing in the lower right corner *(see lower frame, right)*. The ellipse near the top marks the intersection of Beulah and Cole *(upper frame)*, while the arrow marks the spot within the park, on what is now called Martin Luther King, Jr. Drive, where Charlie works on his car *(middle frame)* during the chase, as the rotating sails of the windmill appear in the background through the trees.

The chase concludes *(bottom frame)* with the count's car splashing into the inner lagoon at Fisherman's Wharf, marked with an ellipse *(aerial photo, right)*. This vintage aerial photo predates construction of the Oakland Bay Bridge, which began in 1933. The long diagonal street is Columbus Avenue, leading southeast from the wharf to downtown San Francisco.

This vintage photo, looking east from a spot due north of the end of Jones Street, shows a similar view. The tower at the far left was the old U.S. Customs House, adjacent to the U.S. Immigration Department boarding house to its immediate right. The center building was a fish market. A Pacific Gas & Electric natural gas holding tank, located on the southwest corner of Powell and Jefferson, looms in the back.

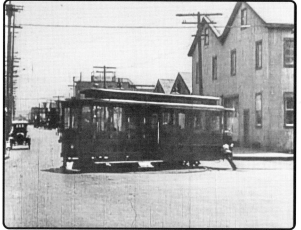

Buster Keaton filmed scenes in San Francisco for his 1922 short, *Daydreams*, a few blocks from where Chaplin filmed. This frame *(right)* looks east at the Powell-Mason cable car turnaround located at Bay and Powell; the companion photo *(left)* was taken in 1937, before the turntable was moved out of the busy intersection. During the scene, Buster fails to notice when the car reverses direction, leading him back towards the police who are chasing him.

Chaplin filmed at Fisherman's Wharf *(lower ellipse)*, while Keaton filmed at the cable car turntable *(upper ellipse)* a few blocks away. This aerial detail reveals the large natural gas holding tank visible in the Chaplin frame on the prior page.

This photo shows Fisherman's Wharf from the same spot today. Landmark restaurants Fisherman's Grotto, Alioto's and Tarantino's now appear in the background.

The Tramp

Released April 12, 1915

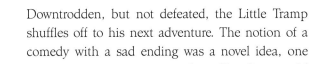

Forever known as the Little Tramp, Chaplin plays his signature role in this early film. Charlie rescues a farmer's daughter (Edna) from a group of hobos, and is offered work as reward. When the thieves return to rob the farmhouse, Charlie foils them again, only to be accidentally shot in the leg. As he convalesces, Charlie falls in love with Edna, but when he learns that she has a sweetheart, he returns to the open road.

In the opening shot, Charlie dodges a speeding car while tramping along a dusty road *(upper left)*. The traffic sign to the left and the two slim white trees to the right in the upper frame *(ellipses)* appear in the concluding scene as well, establishing that both the opening and closing were filmed along the same stretch of road.

Downtrodden, but not defeated, the Little Tramp shuffles off to his next adventure. The notion of a comedy with a sad ending was a novel idea, one that Chaplin would continue to explore. The iconic image of Charlie traipsing away down a lonesome road, with his back to the camera, is one of the most poignant and enduring images of cinema history.

This landmark scene was filmed along Niles Canyon Road, a little further west from where Chaplin filmed the opening shot. This fade-out also marks the end of Chaplin's film career at Niles in Northern California. Frustrated with the facilities and its backwoods location, Chaplin would complete his Essanay contract in Southern California, taking most of his crew with him.

Gerald Smith discovered this setting. The scene was shot looking east down Niles Canyon Road, a bit west of the blue emergency phone sign number 125, east of Niles. The first transcontinental railroad, joined by a golden spike at Promontory Point, Utah, in 1869, ran along Niles Canyon and through Niles before turning north to Oakland and the San Francisco Bay. Today volunteers from the Niles Canyon Railway operate vintage excursion trains along the same track most Sundays of the year.

By the Sea

Released April 29, 1915

Following a brief stint filming in Chicago, and in Niles, California, Chaplin insisted on completing the remainder of his Essanay contract in Los Angeles. *By the Sea* was Chaplin's first Essanay film produced in Southern California, marking his cinematic return since leaving the Keystone Studio at the end of 1914. An improvised amusement park comedy set at the beach, *By the Sea* records the chaos that ensues when Charlie becomes involved with two different couples.

By the Sea was filmed along Ocean Front Walk and the Abbott Kinney Pier in Venice. This aerial photo *(right)* shows the pier just days before it was destroyed by a fire on December 20, 1920. Following a heroic, but ultimately failed effort to save the structure, the pier was rebuilt at tremendous cost, and reopened on July 4, 1921, with a grand ceremony presided over by California Governor William Stevens. The roller coaster along side the lagoon towards the top is the Race Thru the Clouds coaster appearing in the opening shots of *Kid Auto Races*. The directional arrow, corresponding to the arrow in the movie frame, lies near the Venice Plunge, a large saltwater bathhouse.

Actor Billy Armstrong throttles Charlie *(center)* near the Venice Plunge, looking south towards the Abbott Kinney Pier. The trestle-like structure in the upper left of the frame is part of the Venice Scenic Railway built in 1910. On this early style of roller coaster, a brakeman rode along to slow the cars down on the curves while the passengers passed through mountain-like scenery. It was already partially dismantled in the aerial photo.

This pre-1910 photo *(lower right)* shows a similar view before the pier was fully developed.

By the Sea   79

Ballroom dancing was a popular seaside activity. This view, taken between 1906 and 1910, shows the Venice Plunge facing Ocean Front Walk, and the arch-trussed roof *(box)* of the Venice Dance Pavilion, the largest dance hall on the Pacific coast. Hastily erected during the month of June, an army of 125 carpenters completed the hall in time for its July 4, 1906 dedication. The nearly 15,000-square-foot dance floor could easily accommodate 800 dancing couples, while thousands more could watch from its spacious balconies.

Behind Edna, from left to right, we see the Dance Pavilion *(box)*, the crow's nests of the Ship Cafe Restaurant within the box, the midway Ferris wheel near Edna's head, and to the right, the Venice Auditorium.

This view, looking south, shows most of the northern length of the Abbott Kinney Pier. The box *(left)* marks the position of the Venice Plunge discussed on the next page.

Charlie stands poised with a freshly peeled banana, moments before he trips himself on it.

This tourist brochure touts the popular "Balloon Route" of the Los Angeles Pacific Railroad, which carried tourists on a scenic trip counterclockwise from downtown Los Angeles through Hollywood, to the Santa Monica, Venice, and Redondo beaches, and then back to Los Angeles via Culver City. When viewed on a map looking east, the route vaguely resembled the outline of a hot air balloon. Local ads touted "a hundred miles for a hundred cents—one whole day for a dollar."

The ellipse marks Charlie's relative position in the movie frame (above). He is standing by the Venice Diamond Cafe (named Lobel's Cafe at the time of this photo), one of the commercial storefronts housed in the north end of the Venice Plunge complex. I had actively sought out this spot for some time, searching through city directories and dozens of Venice photos, until I somehow spotted this photograph online. I later found a 1915 directory listing confirming the site.

Harold Lloyd's amusement park comedy *Number Please* (1920) was filmed at a number of different parks along the coast. This view looks south down Ocean Front Walk towards the Waldorf Hotel *(left rectangle, see next page)* across from the Venice Plunge *(right rectangle)*, as Harold hopes to sneak past some watchful police by disguising his height with a child perched atop his shoulders.

While several buildings along Ocean Front remain standing today, the pier succumbed to mounting costs and dwindling attendance, and closed in 1947, shortly before it was destroyed by yet another fire. The Venice Plunge closed in 1943, and was demolished in 1947.

This 1908 view shows the east side of the Venice Plunge facing Ocean Front at Market. The Plunge was the largest heated saltwater pool on the West Coast. The section to the right between the two towers housed a hotel, shops, and restaurants, including the corner cafe where Charlie stood *(see rectangle on inset, left)*.

The Plunge was the setting for Buster Keaton's calamitous swim date with Marceline Day in his 1928 MGM feature *The Cameraman*, and was the likely spot where Chaplin filmed the water rescue scene from *The Adventurer*. Kitty-corner from this spot to the left, Chaplin and three boys filmed a deleted street scene for the opening of *Shoulder Arms*.

Caught in a stiff breeze, Charlie and a gentleman struggle to keep their hats perched on their heads. They and their elastic-tethered hats will soon become completely entangled.

Today, the open corner is enclosed within the sliding glass doors of a beach novelty store. I am certain Charlie would be amused by the suggestive T-shirts and towels on display. I knew from studying vintage photos that only a few white buildings stood facing the beach front north of Venice, and photos such as the one below convinced me that the spot was likely the Waldorf Hotel, on the northeast corner of Ocean Front and Westminster. Visiting in person confirmed the site, and I was pleased to see little has changed after 90 years.

The Waldorf Hotel was built in 1913, and still exudes a stately presence along Ocean Front Walk in Venice.

Photos such as this, as well as other views looking north up Ocean Front Walk from the Venice Plunge, helped me to pinpoint the film's setting. Notice the open-cornered, white-tiled Waldorf near the center of the photo.

Charlie flirts with Edna beside a park bench located on Palisades Park in Santa Monica. Behind Charlie are handrails for a stairway leading down the face of the bluff. These stairs could be the ones leading down to the beach *(top ellipse)* on the adjoining vintage aerial photo of the bluff-top park.

Harold Lloyd approves an artist's handiwork at Palisades Park in his 1921 short film, *A Sailor-Made Man*.

Buster Keaton used the same setting to film this dramatic interlude for the opening of his 1923 short, *The Love Nest*. Notice the rustic, gnarled branch railings, a distinctive feature, in all three frames.

A vintage view of Palisades Park, similar to the view in the film.

The LAPRR Balloon Route stopped at a station *(square)* located in the park. The lower ellipse shows train tracks leading onto the beach from a tunnel at a spot where today the Santa Monica Freeway opens onto the Pacific Coast Highway.

A view of the southeast corner of Speedway and Horizon, today virtually unchanged.

Billy Armstrong runs into a meddlesome cop before a house at the southeast corner of Speedway and Horizon in Venice. I found this location with some educated guesswork and luck. Assuming the shot looks east away from the ocean, the foreground fireplug would be sitting on a northeast corner, with the background houses sitting a few lots further east.

Checking the Sanborn fire insurance maps, Ocean Front had a few northeast corner fireplugs, while an alley, Speedway, ran parallel to Ocean Front a few lots to the east. Assuming Charlie did not stray far for this shot, I simply checked spots between Ocean Front and Speedway, and quickly found this site one block to the south of the Waldorf. This corner was only a half-block due east of the Venice Diamond Cafe discussed earlier.

A close-up view of the frame reveals various window and trim details.

A closer view shows the same details.

Looking to the northeast, this aerial photo of Venice predates 1920, as the Venice Scenic Railway (1910, replaced by the Big Dipper coaster in 1920) appears at the bottom left of the photo. The upper right frame is from *Kid Auto Races* while the lower right frame is from *Shoulder Arms*. The arrows suggest the compass direction of the movie camera taking each frame. The top two frames were shot looking west and south, and the bottom three frames were shot looking south, east, and west, respectively.

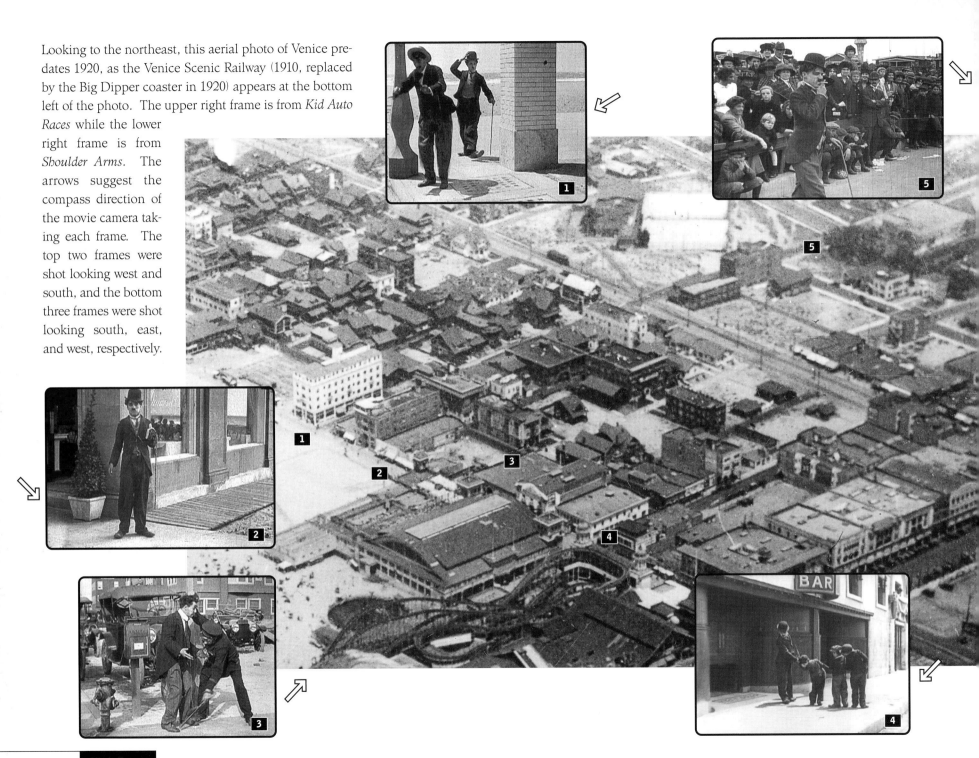

Work

A ssistant paper-hanger Charlie hauls his boss and their work cart up a steep hill to their customer's home. Distracted by a pretty maid (Edna), Charlie's efforts lead to predictably messy results.

Having moved from the Majestic Studio facilities, Chaplin filmed *Work* within the Bradbury mansion at 147 North Hill Street on the corner of Court Street, first used as a studio in 1913. This circa-1890 view *(right)* shows the mansion at the top of Court Hill. The movie frame *(lower left)* shows Charlie arriving at the steps of the mansion. The ellipse in each image marks Chaplin's spot.

In *Making a Living (middle)*, Charlie ran down Broadway from the corner of First, past the L.A. Times Building. This 1925 aerial view shows the proximity of the Bradbury mansion setting *(ellipse)* to the Times building corner *(arrow)*. The small rectangle marks the distinctive twin-bore Hill Street Tunnel under Court Hill. The large rectangle marks the future site of the present-day City Hall, which opened in 1928.

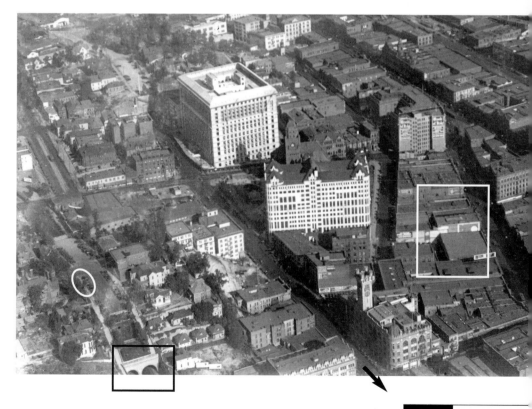

This view shows the steps of the Bradbury mansion as they appeared in the film.

For a time, comedian Harold Lloyd worked with comedy producer Hal Roach at the Rolin Studios, located in the Bradbury mansion. It was here, in 1915, that Lloyd devised his Lonesome Luke character. Lloyd would later describe the mansion's large, drafty rooms as "pneumonia hall." In this photo, Harold appears by the sidewalk steps in front of the mansion during a scene from *Count Your Change* (1919).

The Bradbury mansion was one of the finest homes in town. As the city expanded, the wealthy moved farther out, and formerly prosperous neighborhoods fell into decline. Before it was demolished in 1929, the mansion was used as a number of

apartments and artist's lofts. It also contained a restaurant frequented by the Superior Court judges who would take the Court Flight railway up for lunch from the courthouse below. A reporter described climbing up each floor of the house, via diminishingly grand staircases, to the uppermost tower, affording one of the most spectacular views in town. The sidewalk wall detail *(rectangle)* matches the detail behind Harold Lloyd *(above right)*.

The carved panels beside the porch *(inset)* match the movie frame *(above, left)*.

The Los Angeles Civic Center was built among a series of small hills interlaced by a number of short tunnels. The Second and Third Street Tunnels ran east–west underneath Bunker Hill, while two tunnels ran off of Broadway beneath Fort Moore Hill. The Hill Street Tunnel was barely a half-block long, running under Court Hill from First Street to the south and Temple Street to the north.

Originally constructed with one bore, its unique twin-bore design was a city landmark for decades. Trolleys used the left tunnel, autos the right. You can see three rails because different gauge trolley lines used the same tunnel; the two outer rails served the wide gauge cars, while an interior rail and an outer rail served narrow gauge cars. The dead-end bluff overlooking the Hill Street Tunnel made an ideal movie location *(see* Shoulder Arms*)*.

This view north is from the 1940s.

Court Hill, and the distinctive twin bores of the Hill Street Tunnel, appear behind Bobby Dunn dancing on a rooftop in *Hot Foot* (1924).

A traffic cops stands before the south end of the Hill Street Tunnel at the First Street intersection. Notice that the short tunnel does not begin until nearly half-way up the block.

Footsore travelers could avoid climbing the 140 steps up from Broadway to Hill Street by taking the Court Hill Railway, the city's second funicular railway, built in 1905. Half as short, and nearly twice as steep as Angel's Flight, it claimed to be the world's shortest railway. An observation tower stood at the top of the hill offering one of the finest views in town. Chaplin, Harold Lloyd, and all the other movie people working atop Court Hill undoubtedly took this train downhill during lunch breaks.

Originally, the elite Court Hill residents would take the railway down to Broadway for shopping and errands, while in later years workers would leave their cars at hilltop parking lots where beautiful Victorian mansions had once stood, and take the railway to their office jobs below.

Sam Vandergrift single-handedly ran the railway, often for 15 hours a day, for nearly 28 years, taking off only three days to get married. Sam was so dedicated to his service he reportedly never saw a motion picture or attended a ball game. After Sam's death in 1932, his widow, Annie, struggled to keep the line operating until she was finally granted permission to abandon the public franchise in 1943. Flames ravaged the line a few months later, and by 1955, the hill upon which the rail line had operated was completely excavated. Annie died in 1967, at age 86. Sam and Annie's lifetime of quiet service somehow touched me, and I am glad to honor them briefly here.

The Court Hill Railway's more famous sister, Angel's Flight, opened in 1901 beside the Third Street Tunnel at Hill Street. It was torn down in 1969, only to be

reopened, a half-block away, in 1996. It was closed once again in 2001 after a faulty cable gear mechanism broke, causing one of the cars to crash into the other, killing one person and injuring seven. Angel's Flight is currently being restored and re-built, with plans to re-open in late-2006.

Harold Lloyd also filmed atop Court Hill at the Bradbury mansion. This unidentified scene from a Lloyd film appears to have been taken at the same corner where Charlie pulls his work cart into view.

This aerial view shows the house at the northeast corner of Court and Hill opposite from the Bradbury mansion.

This movie frame *(upper right)* looks from the Bradbury mansion to the Hopperstead home on the diagonal corner. Built in 1880, the unique hilltop house had a large second-floor balcony on three sides of the home. Mrs. Rachel Hopperstead successfully enjoined the construction of the Court Flight railway for several months until her demands were satisfied. The second-floor window *(ellipse)* in the frame corresponds to the window in this photo *(right)*. The house and the rest of Court Hill were all demolished in 1955.

This 1930s-era map *(right)* shows how the short Hill Street Tunnel ran from First Street to Temple. The dark rectangle marks the location of the Bradbury mansion.

In 1955, the Hill Street Tunnel was demolished, and much of Court Hill was excavated. The rectangle in the two bottom photos shows the approximate location of the former Bradbury mansion. If you were to stand on Hill Street today, the Bradbury site would be several stories up in the air! The site is now part of the Civic Center Mall (1966), officially known as the El Paseo

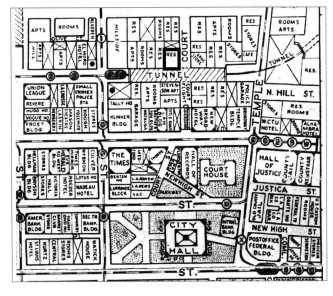

Pobladores de Los Angeles, or "The Walk of the First Settlers of Los Angeles." It honors the 44 settlers from Mexico, led by Filipe de Neve, who founded Los Angeles on September 4, 1781.

The mall rests above a large underground parking lot, and is bounded by the Los Angeles County Superior Court on First Street to the left, and the Kenneth Hahn Hall of Administration on Temple Street to the right. Today, the downtown Los Angeles Civic Center boasts the largest concentration of local, state, and federal government buildings of any city outside of Washington, D.C.

A Woman

Released July 12, 1915

In this "park" comedy, Charlie enrages two men when he disrupts their flirtations with a young lady. Charlie befriends the wife and daughter of one of the men, and visits the ladies at their home. When the angry men later arrive at the home, Charlie escapes by disguising himself as a woman. The two men flirt shamelessly with Charlie, only to discover his secret and chase him out the door.

The movie was filmed at Lincoln Park, located east of North Mission Road and north of Valley Boulevard, a few miles northeast of downtown.

A similar view taken in 1924.

Charlie strolls through Lincoln Park, its distinctive boat house barely visible in the background.

Originally dedicated as East Los Angeles Park in 1881, the park was renamed Eastlake Park in 1901, and later renamed again as Lincoln Park in 1917. The park's first sculpture, depicting Lincoln as a young lawyer, was dedicated on July 4, 1926. In 1911, pioneer filmmaker William Selig built a private zoo and movie studios for his Selig Polyscope Company just north of the park, on a street today named Selig Place.

The Selig Zoo Park, touted as the world's largest private zoo, celebrated its grand opening June 20, 1915, at about the time Chaplin filmed at Eastlake. A popular ostrich farm and alligator farm were also located across from the park on the west side of Mission Road. Selig filmed *The Power of the Sultan* in 1908, reportedly the first film shot entirely in Southern California, on a small rented lot next to a Chinese laundry on Olive Street.

Leaping from a bridge, Harold Lloyd's attempt to drown himself in *Haunted Spooks* (1920) is thwarted by the deceptively shallow water of Lincoln Park's pond.

This 1924 photo matches the movie frame above. The box marks the approximate spot on the park green where Chaplin filmed the scene on the preceding page.

This tracking shot taken from Roscoe Arbuckle's *When Love Took Wings* (1915) was filmed moving west along Valley Boulevard towards Mission Road.

Looking north, this frame to the right shows Chaplin leading actor Charles Insley along the east edge of the Lincoln Park pond. The shrubbery by the water's edge *(circle)* matches the shrubbery behind Chaplin in the earlier shot *(left)*.

The same view today. A modern boat launch ramp now appears in the foreground.

This portrait was taken during the filming of *A Woman* on July 2, 1915.

There is nothing inherently comic about Buster Keaton's subdued but convincing portrayal *(bottom right)* as the "wife" in his 1921 short film, *The Playhouse*. The humor lies in realizing that both members of this seemingly ordinary "couple" are played by the same person. Conversely, Keaton's drag performance in *Backstage* (1919) *(bottom center)* is funny because Buster makes no effort to disguise his masculinity.

While Chaplin also played an obviously male "female" character in *A Busy Day* (1914) *(lower left)*, his convincing drag impersonation in *A Woman* forms the centerpiece of the movie. Chaplin's lingering close-ups of himself in drag, flirting with the camera, are more than a bit disturbing. The film was even reported to have been banned for several years in Sweden. Chaplin also played a convincing female in *The Masquerader* (1914) *(upper left)*.

Charlie plays a bank janitor who stores his mop and cleaning supplies within the sturdy vault. Charlie mistakes bank teller Edna's gift to another man as a token of her love for Charlie. Crestfallen when he learns the truth, Charlie dreams of heroically rescuing Edna from bank robbers and receiving her kiss in gratitude, only to find himself caressing a mop upon awakening. With its sorrowful ending, *The Bank* highlights Chaplin's developing skill at blending comedy and pathos.

When Lobster Films/Kino International released Harold Lloyd's *His Royal Slyness* (1920) on DVD, I somehow noticed this shot of Harold departing from a taxi. The building visible in the background clearly matches the distinctive features of the Chaplin frame. Note the matching horizontal details on the façade, the position of the wall lamp, and the square grillwork details along the window bottoms.

In this opening shot, Charlie strolls to work in front of the Trinity Auditorium located at 851 South Grand. One reason this setting was so hard to find was that I had incorrectly limited my search to real banks. I found this spot quite by chance while poring over vintage downtown photos.

I then noticed this shot from Harold Lloyd's *Bumping Into Broadway* (1919). Not only does the background match the Chaplin frame, it also reveals how the buildings appeared looking farther down the street from where Chaplin had filmed.

The ellipse marks Charlie's position relative to the far lantern *(square)* in each shot.

The Trinity Auditorium Building, later known as the Embassy, is located at 851 South Grand Street near Ninth Street. The first three stories were dedicated to the Trinity Church, while the upper six floors housed a men's dormitory containing 330 rooms and a rooftop garden capped by a 70-foot-diameter dome.

The complex featured a library, a gymnasium, tennis and handball courts, a cafeteria, a cafe, and a barbershop. The church's goal was to satisfy the requirements of mind, body, and soul. "We can take a man from the shower bath to the pearly gates," the Rev. C.C. Selecman said a day before the complex opened. The 2,500-seat, three-tier auditorium, with elegant reception halls, and a banquet hall that could seat 1,000, was once the center of Los Angeles culture.

Construction began November 13, 1913, capped by a September 21, 1914 opening night concert featuring basso opera singer Juan de la Cruz. The Los Angeles Philharmonic, the city's first permanent symphony orchestra, made its debut here in 1919, playing Dvorzak's *New World Symphony*. By the 1930s the hall was known as the Embassy, a celebrated venue for jazz concerts featuring Duke Ellington and Count Basie, while rock concerts played here in the 1960s.

In recent years, the Embassy was acquired by USC for use as a resident annex. Located in the burgeoning South Park entertainment district, a few blocks from the massive Los Angeles Convention Center and Staples Center complex, the Embassy was acquired by the Gansevoort Hotel Group with plans to give it a $30 million makeover, converting the hotel and auditorium into an upscale destination for young and affluent patrons.

On July 22, 1915, about the same time that Chaplin filmed here, William Jennings Bryan, famed lecturer and former Secretary of State to Woodrow Wilson, delivered a stirring oratory about "Man's Duty to Government, to Society, and to God." Bryan was perhaps most famous for prosecuting the Scopes "Monkey Trial" in 1925.

Looking north up Grand Avenue. The building today looks essentially unchanged.

A full view, matching the *Bumping into Broadway* frame.

Until 1957, the city was subject to a 150-foot, 13-story height restriction—the lone exception being Los Angeles City Hall, at 28 stories, which opened in 1928. This vintage 1986 view gives some idea of the remarkable transformation of the city's skyline that has since transpired. Today, even more towering structures fill the sky. The arrow marks Chaplin's path.

Work was Chaplin's last Essanay project completed at the Bradbury mansion. In June 1915, Chaplin and company moved to larger quarters at the rented Majestic Studios located at 651 Fairview Avenue in Boyle Heights, where *The Bank* was filmed. The site was later home to the Liberty Film Company. This wonderful shot shows most of the cast and crew during production. Notice the muslin light diffusers hanging over the open-air stage. David Kiehn's book *Broncho Billy and the Essanay Film Company* identifies nearly every person in this shot.

This detail (*left*) shows Charlie and Edna to the right of producer Jess Robbins. Behind them is the bank teller set, seen in use in the frame above. If you look closely, Jess Robbins appears at both ends of the panorama shot above. As the camera slowly panned from left to right during the exposure, Robbins simply strolled behind the camera to join the other end of the line.

These twin frames show the bank's inner and outer office set where much of the action takes place. The corresponding part of the set lies directly beneath, revealing that the "wall" separating the two sets was nearly paper thin.

The bank vault, checkerboard floor tiles, and staircase evident in this movie frame appear in the photo below.

Police

Released from prison, Charlie meets a corrupt preacher who picks his pocket while encouraging Charlie to go straight. (Although unidentified, the industrial building Chaplin used as a prison at the beginning of *Police* (*upper right*) was used similarly in the 1919 Hank Mann comedy *The Janitor*, available through UnknownVideo.com.) Lacking money, Charlie is evicted from a flophouse, only to be held up by a robber. The robber convinces Charlie to join him in burglarizing Edna's house. When the police arrive, Edna protects Charlie by telling the police he is her husband.

Although tempted himself, Charlie realizes that a corrupt preacher has already stolen this drunken man's watch (*right*). Charlie is standing in front of the Chin Woo building in the heart of old Chinatown. The same building appears in the background of this frame showing Jackie Coogan in *The Kid*. The arrow in each image points to the same entryway facing Juan Street.

This vintage view of the Chin Woo building (*lower right*) looks south down Juan Street to the left, and west down Apablasa to the right. The ellipse marks where Chaplin stood at the corner of the building. The building's distinctive horizontal brick detailing caught my eye after I had remembered seeing it in *The Kid*.

Charlie assesses a suspicious second preacher before taking a swing at him. They are standing beneath the awning of a very old building, at some type of unusual "T"- or "L"-intersection across from an 843 street address, presumably near the plaza where two other related scenes were filmed. The white building in the background stands flush with the sidewalk, while the 843 building is set well back from the sidewalk.

Based on these clues, I believe this shot was taken looking west beside a saloon located at the tip of where Alameda Street terminates by merging into Spring Street. Searching the area using old aerial photos and the highly detailed Sanborn fire insurance maps, the location at the north tip of Alameda Street exactly fits all of the above clues, and appears to be unique among settings relatively near the plaza. The arrow pointing west on this 1920 Baist Atlas map *(lower left)* represents the camera's point of view for the shot. Notice how the 843 building sits back from the street, while its neighbor to the left is flush with the street. To the right of 843 was a paper warehouse for the Times Mirror Company, the publisher of the *Los Angeles Times* newspaper.

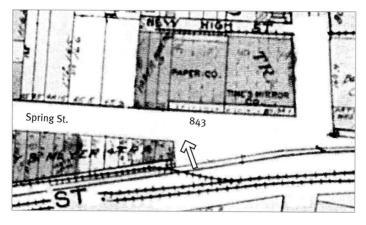

(1) Charlie swings at a preacher and chases him south down Spring Street from Alameda, (2) then north up New High Street towards the corner of Republic Street, then (3) around the corner from south on Spring Street to east down Ord Street, as shown on this vintage view taken looking north from City Hall.

The preacher turns back for a moment to look at Charlie chasing him. The arrow in all four images points to the back of the Brunswig Drug Company building at the northeast corner of New High and Republic. The drug company building appears in the opening shot of Chaplin's later film, *A Dog's Life* (1918).

Today, most of New High Street has been buried by parking lots and subsumed by other streets. But the Brunswig Building still stands, facing Main Street across from the Pico House, and a stone's throw from the plaza.

Looking north, the doglegged street to the left is New High Street. The straight street to the right is Main Street, passing across the west (*left*) side of the plaza. The cupola towers of the Baker Building on Main Street (*discussed in* The Kid) appear to the lower right.

This reaction shot of policemen chasing Harold Lloyd appears in his 1920 short *Hand to Mouth*, which is discussed further in the *A Dog's Life* chapter. Much of Lloyd's film was shot along New High Street north of the plaza.

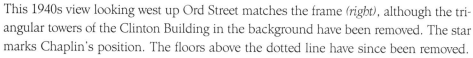

This 1940s view looking west up Ord Street matches the frame *(right)*, although the triangular towers of the Clinton Building in the background have been removed. The star marks Chaplin's position. The floors above the dotted line have since been removed.

Charlie chases the preacher past a wall reading "*****sino Wine Company." Elizabeth Foote searched city directories to confirm this was the Aquilino Largomarsino Wine Company located at 109 Ord Street. Notice the crowd of bystanders *(box)* in the background. In 1917, a

year after Chaplin filmed here, the Anti-Saloon League convinced Los Angeles voters to adopt local prohibition (two years before the federal prohibition), presumably putting this winery out of business. The open fields east of the plaza were originally vineyards owned by Juan Apablasa, discussed in *Caught in a Cabaret.*

Looking west up Ord from Alameda, we see the upper floors of the Clinton and Largomarsino buildings to the far left have been removed. Chaplin was walking towards the future home of Philippe The Original, a landmark Los Angeles restaurant established in 1908 by Philippe Mathieu, that claims to have invented the "French Dipped Sandwich." The restaurant operated from its original location on Aliso Street until 1951, when construction of the Santa Ana Freeway caused it to move to its present location.

This 1938 sketch by *Los Angeles Times* artist Charles Owens shows a similar view.

This view *(left)* looks north toward the south side of the Clinton Building from New High Street. Located near the plaza, a dilapidated adobe dwelling stands in the foreground.

To the right, Chaplin's best friend, the swashbuckling silent film star Douglas Fairbanks, performs a stunt high atop a telephone pole in front of the Clinton Building in his 1916 film, *The Matrimaniac*. It is likely Chaplin and Fairbanks never suspected that the same building appeared in both of their 1916 films.

This 1930s aerial view *(bottom)* shows Chaplin's position *(ellipse)* as he walked to the right down Ord Street towards the Phillipe building on Alameda Street. Ord Street was named for Lieut. Edward O.C. Ord, who conducted the first American survey of the pueblo in 1849, after the Mexican War, and later served as a general in the Civil War. Fort Ord in Monterey, California, is named for him. For his map, Ord selected the front door of the Plaza Church on Main Street (then Calle Principal) as the geographic center of the city. It is rumored that Spring Street (then Calle Primavera) was named for Ord's love, whom he had nicknamed *Mi Primavera* ("My Springtime").

This view looks north up Main Street towards the plaza, with the Baker Building cupola towers in the foreground. The rectangle marks the same corner of Sanchez and Arcadia.

These photos help set the stage for the location where Charlie is robbed as described on the next page. This 1920s aerial view looks east over the plaza. Main Street runs across the bottom of the plaza, Los Angeles Street runs across the top of the plaza. Sanchez is the narrow alley, between Main and Los Angeles, running from the right side of the plaza. The rectangle marks the back corner of the Hotel de Paris at Sanchez and Arcadia.

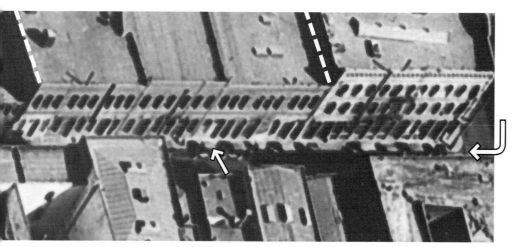

This detail shows block-long Sanchez Street. The curved arrow indicates where Buster Keaton rounds the corner from Arcadia onto Sanchez in his 1920 short film, *Neighbors (right)*. Between the dotted lines stand the Garnier Building, and to its right, the Hotel de Paris. The small arrow points to 413 Sanchez, discussed on the next page.

A cop leads Buster from Arcadia onto Sanchez past the corner of the Hotel de Paris. The 1906 Sanborn fire insurance maps explain that the upper floors of this hotel were used for "female boarding," a euphemism for a bordello. The square post held aloft one of the carbon-arc street lamps installed downtown in the 1880s.

A robber futilely searches Charlie's pockets while Charlie helps himself to the robber's wallet. I believe this was filmed at the back of the Garnier Building, current home of the Chinese American Museum, along the east side of Sanchez. The ellipse in each image marks the back of 413 Sanchez.

Jackie Coogan appears in *My Boy* (1921) rushing down Sanchez. The narrow doorway behind him (413½ Sanchez) was originally a window. *My Boy* contains many shots along the length of Sanchez, a valuable tool for piecing the clues together.

This montage from Keaton's *Neighbors* was filmed at the same spot Chaplin used in *Police*. If you study the door panels, window ledges, brick details, the wire and wood window screens, the sidewalk skylights, and below-grade window arches, they all match precisely with the Chaplin frame.

In *The Kid*, Chaplin rides a truck from a private alley onto Arcadia Street, with a view north up Sanchez visible in the background.

Consisting of eight individual units, the Garnier Building was built in 1890 specifically for lease to Chinese merchants, with ground-floor shops and upper-floor apartments. The back of each unit originally had a central door, with a window to each side, creating a regular sequence of windows and doors: W-D-W, W-D-W, etc. According to the Sanborn fire insurance maps, sometime between 1894 and 1906,

unit 413 was subdivided into two units, 413 and 413½ , by creating a narrow back door from one of the window openings. This narrow door appears behind Jackie Coogan on the preceding page. This reconfigured doorway disrupts the normal sequence because it is the only place where two doors (D-D) appear side by side.

This tracking shot along Sanchez from Keaton's *Neighbors (above)* shows from left to right a sequence of doors and windows as follows: D-W, W-D-W, narrow D-D-W. This same sequence, including the narrow door, appears in between the dotted lines *(left)* in this frame enlargement of Sanchez from *The Kid*. The protruding window sills and the vertical brick transition *(arrow)* can be seen in all three shots. Based on these and other clues, I am convinced that the setting for this scene from *Police (below)* and the tracking shot from *Neighbors* both appear in this frame *(left)* from *The Kid*, looking up Sanchez from the northeast corner of Arcadia.

This similar view of the corner of Arcadia and Sanchez *(lower right)*, comes from the 1925 Jackie Coogan feature *The Rag Man*, the same spot where Coogan had filmed *The Kid* four years earlier.

This 1920 photo *(left)* looks north up Sanchez from the corner of Arcadia. The trees in the plaza appear at the end of the street. For decades, the Garnier Building was home to Chinese merchants, including one of the first general merchandise stores, the Sun Wing Wo store at No. 419–421, pictured in this 1902 photo *(right)*. These stores provided a sense of community, where local residents could socialize and keep in touch with news from home. Today, many furnishings from this store are displayed at the Chinese American Museum.

Buster Keaton (1922's *Cops*) and Harry Langdon (1927's *Long Pants*) filmed scenes nearby at the corner of Los Angeles and Arcadia *(middle and lower left, see next page)*.

The ellipse in this frame from *My Boy (above)* marks the doorway where Chaplin filmed. The arrow marks the narrow doorway also appearing in this view *(lower right)* south down Sanchez from Harry Langdon's 1924 short film, *Feet of Mud*. The Waterhouse and Lester Wagon Parts and Iron Warehouse building along Arcadia appears behind Harry at the end of the street.

Arcadia Street at the south end of Sanchez Street

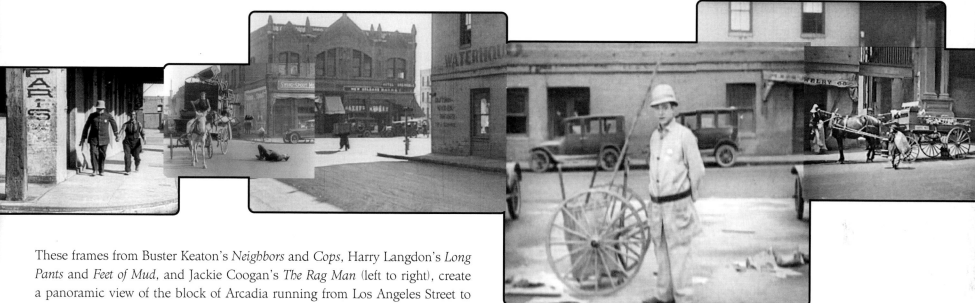

These frames from Buster Keaton's *Neighbors* and *Cops*, Harry Langdon's *Long Pants* and *Feet of Mud*, and Jackie Coogan's *The Rag Man* (left to right), create a panoramic view of the block of Arcadia running from Los Angeles Street to Main. Viewed from left to right we see the Hotel de Paris, at the southeast corner of Sanchez and Arcadia, the intersection of Los Angeles Street and Arcadia, the Waterhouse and Lester building running along Arcadia, and the alley opening at the back of the Baker Building through which Charlie rides the truck in *The Kid*.

Mrs. Arcadia de Baker (born Arcadia Bandini in 1823) was known as the wealthiest woman in Southern California, leaving an estate worth $8 million when she died in 1912. At age 14 Arcadia married her first husband, 40-year-old Abel Stearns, the region's largest rancher and land owner. He built a large adobe for her at Main and Arcadia Streets called El Palacio de Don Abel.

When Stearns died in 1871, Arcadia married Col. Robert S. Baker, the wealthy co-founder of Santa Monica and namesake for Bakersfield. Baker tore down the El Palacio in 1875, and built the magnificent Baker Building *(visible at far right above, see* The Kid *chapter)* in its place. Today, Arcadia's namesake street is little more than an access road running parallel to the freeway.

This 1920s-era photo *(left)* shows the entire length of Sanchez, with the Garnier Building situated between the dashed lines, adjacent to the Hotel de Paris on the right. The section of the Garnier Building to the right of the dotted line and the entire Hotel de Paris were demolished in part to make way for the Santa Ana Freeway. The arrow points to where Chaplin filmed.

This modern view of Sanchez *(lower right)* shows the remaining five out of eight units of the Garnier Building standing today, now home to the Chinese American Museum, and part of the larger El Pueblo de Los Angeles Historic Monument, a collection of 27 historic buildings clustered around the central plaza. The section of three storefronts to the left of the vertical line is unchanged, and is similar in appearance to the section where Chaplin filmed. The center section to the right of the line was completely remodeled with a large door and archway. Unfortunately, the particular spot where Chaplin filmed *(ellipse)* was demolished.

This 1950s view *(lower left)* shows the construction of the Santa Ana Freeway along what was Arcadia Street. Main Street runs north up the left side of the photo, Los Angeles Street runs north to the right. The arrow marks the spot on Sanchez where Chaplin filmed. The Union Train Station, upper right, stands along Alameda where the old Chinatown was once located.

This 1930s view looks north past the City Hall tower towards the plaza and most of the old Chinatown to the right before it was demolished to build the Union Train Station. (1) was filmed at Alameda and Spring, out of frame to the upper left; (2) marks the Largomarsino Wine Company building on Ord Street; (3) points to the corner of Juan and Apablasa Streets, where Charlie is tempted to steal from a drunk; (4) points to Sanchez Street where the holdup scene was filmed; and (5) points to New High Street near the corner of Republic, where the Brunswig Drug Company building appears behind the preacher.

The Lone Star Studio (Mutual)

After his Essanay contract expired, Chaplin signed a contract in 1916 with the Mutual Film Corporation to make a dozen two-reel comedies. His $10,000 weekly salary and $150,000 signing bonus made Chaplin the highest paid entertainer in the world. Mutual provided Chaplin with the old Climax Studio, located at the southwest corner of Lillian Way and Eleanor in Hollywood, and named it the Lone Star Studio in his honor. Chaplin would later describe the time making these Mutual films as the happiest period of his career.

When Chaplin concluded his Mutual contract with the release of *The Adventurer* in 1917, the small studio was taken over by the Metro Studios. A few years later, when Paramount signed Roscoe "Fatty" Arbuckle in 1920 to star in a series of feature films, his partner and protégé, 24-year-old Buster Keaton, was set up with his own production company and assigned the former Lone Star Studio. It was here from 1920 to 1928 that Keaton filmed all of his independently produced shorts and feature films. In a twist that would perhaps make Buster chuckle, a commemorative plaque honoring the site of the Keaton Studio now lies on the wrong corner of the street. The plaque fails to mention that Chaplin had earlier filmed his richly inventive Mutual films here as well.

The highlight of the film involved Charlie's antics on a runaway escalator.

Charlie plays a department store clerk who prevents a dishonest floorwalker and store manager from embezzling funds. The film was Chaplin's first comedy produced for the Mutual company, and marked the first appearance of Chaplin's favorite villain, Scottish-born character actor Eric Campbell, known as Chaplin's "Goliath" for his towering frame and menacing demeanor.

Looking west from Lillian Way, this view shows Chaplin *(inset)* supervising the construction of the department store set on the Lone Star Studio open-air stage. Muslin cloth was suspended on wires overhead to diffuse the direct sunlight when filming.

This detail shows crew members assembling the escalator steps and the parallel forms delineating where the escalator would be built.

The house *(square)* visible in the far background of this photo was located a block away at 1022 Cole Avenue.

By 1920, Buster Keaton would be filming at the same small studio. The house at 1022 Cole Avenue appears behind Keaton in this frame from his 1921 short film, *The Boat*.

1022 Cole Avenue also appears as Buster's girlfriend's house in his 1924 feature film *Sherlock Jr.*

This aerial view shows the open-air stage *(arrow)* and its relation to 1022 Cole Avenue *(square)* in the background. This house, and the rest of the Cole Avenue block across from the studio, would later become the site of the Technicolor Building, which housed the company's headquarters and laboratories from 1930–1975.

Charlie plays a bungling apprentice fireman, frustrating the owner of a burning house who has trouble rousing Charlie and crew to its rescue. Another man sets fire to his house in order to collect insurance, unaware that his daughter (Edna) is trapped upstairs. Charlie clambers up the side of the house to rescue her and saves the day.

The Fireman was Chaplin's second film shot at his new studio. He conveniently filmed several scenes close by. These two photographs show the studio office located on the southwest corner of Lillian Way and Eleanor. They were taken at a time when Metro controlled the small studio, after Chaplin had left in 1917, but before Buster Keaton arrived to use the studio in 1920.

This view of the studio *(below)* looking to the southwest reveals a series of vertical posts alongside the open-air stage that were used to support sheets of muslin to diffuse the sunlight. The ellipse marks a small sloped shed, and the transition of a tall fence to a short fence along Lillian, that appear on the next page.

A group of visitors *(left)* poses on the south side of the open-air stage to the left. Chaplin's half-brother Syd is at the far left.

This view *(right)* looks east along the south side of the open-air stage. Notice the matching vertical posts. The ellipse in the background contains a small sloped shed, and a transition from a tall fence to a short fence, along Lillian Way, as highlighted on the previous page.

This group photo *(lower left)* was also shot on the south side of the open-air stage.

This view *(below)*, showing the south side of the studio running along Romaine, was taken after Chaplin left the studio in 1917. The ellipse marks the open corner of the studio where Chaplin built the burning-house set and house-rescue set for *The Fireman*, and the tenement set for *Easy Street*. At the time Chaplin filmed here, this corner of the studio was not yet fenced off. The arrow points to the relative spot Chaplin is standing in the above photo.

Many comic scenes were filmed at the corner of the studio, looking south down Lillian Way. The left arrow marks the porch of the Congregational Sunday School. The right arrow marks the chimneys of the Vine Street Public School.

The Congregational Sunday School porch appears in this opening shot from Buster Keaton's 1920 short film, *One Week (left)*. In this scene from *Sherlock Jr.* (1924) *(right)*, Buster practices his sleuthing skills by trailing a suspicious character. They walk across Lillian Way past the corner of the studio. Several more buildings are evident than when Chaplin filmed here eight years earlier.

This frame shows the studio corner, including the Lillian Way/Eleanor street sign.

This modern view matches the frame to the left. Today, a nondescript warehouse-style building occupies the site. A plaque in the foreground commemorating the Keaton Studio sits on the wrong corner. The plaque also fails to mention that this studio site was once home to Chaplin during his Mutual period. As a silent comedy

fan, I was amazed to learn that Chaplin and Keaton had once shared the same studio "home," and remain amazed that this remarkable coincidence is not more widely known today.

This frame from *The Fireman* shows the fire wagon traveling south down Lillian Way towards the Vine Street Public School.

Later in Keaton's *Sherlock, Jr.*, Buster rides on the handlebars of a driverless motorcycle up Lillian Way past the school towards Eleanor. The studio is to the immediate right of the frame.

The firemen fight a burning house set *(above)*. The production seems to have attracted quite a crowd of onlookers *(right)*. This view looks to the southwest from the corner of the studio located at Romaine and Cahuenga. The small cabin in the background *(rectangle)*, located at 1007 Cahuenga, would appear in three of Buster Keaton's films *(below)*.

This scene from Keaton's 1920 short film *The Scarecrow* shows actor Big Joe Roberts tipping over a tin lizzie. The cabin appears in the background between the two men. The house at the far left was built after the photo *(above)* was taken.

This scene is from Keaton's 1927 feature, *College*, as Buster grabs a laundry pole in order to vault into his girl's dormitory room.

This scene from Keaton's 1928 feature, *Steamboat Bill, Jr.*, shows Buster standing within the studio fence, the same house and cabin in the background.

This stunt-climbing set *(left)* was built on the same spot as the burning-house set on the corner of Romaine and Cahuenga, looking south from Romaine. The rectangle in the background marks the location of four homes on Cole Avenue that appear in another Chaplin frame *(below, middle)*.

This composite view *(right)* depicts Chaplin performing an impressive stunt as he climbs the three-story set in one continuous take.

The first of these four houses, 817 Cole, also appeared behind Buster as he constructed a home in his 1920 short, *One Week*.

The inset from the above photo shows houses located at 817, 833, 837, and 843 Cole Avenue. The same four houses appear in this later shot from the film *(middle)*.

Looking south, this aerial photo of the Keaton Studio (the small square block in the foreground), was likely taken on March 7, 1921. The corner of Lillian Way and Eleanor touching the bottom edge is where Chaplin filmed scenes from *The Fireman* five years earlier. The + marks the studio's open-air stage, and the star marks the corner of Cahuenga and Romaine. The two large center blocks across from the Keaton Studio are crammed with the offices, stages, and outdoor sets of the Metro Film Company that would become part of Metro-Goldwyn-Meyer in 1924. When Chaplin filmed *The Fireman* here in 1916, these two center blocks were essentially vacant lots. The rectangle marks where the four houses on Cole Avenue, identified on the prior page, were located.

The sets from four films, from top to bottom: *The Fireman*, *The Fireman* again, *Easy Street*, Buster Keaton's *Neighbors*, and Keaton's *The Boat*; all were filmed in the same studio corner marked with a star. Buster would build many other sets at this site.

Charlie races to a fire drill.

Chaplin relaxes with Eric Campbell. A crew member holding a clipboard stands in the foreground.

A full view of Station No. 29.

Chaplin filmed at Fire Station No. 29 located at 158 S. Western, now the home of a carpet store and a Korean bridal shop. The station opened on April 16, 1913, and would remain in use until 1988, the longest continuously-used fire station in Los Angeles. In 1913, Hollywood was so new and remote that it was not even hooked up to the municipal water system. The Los Angeles Aqueduct, engineered by William Mulholland to bring water from the Owens Valley, opened later that year. The ready access to plentiful water helped fuel the phenomenal growth that took place in Los Angeles during the 1920s and '30s.

This vintage view *(right)* looks north up Western. The station tower appears by the right telephone pole.

Taken a bit further north on Western, a similar view north past Fire Station House No. 29 *(below)*.

Charlie races up Western from Fire Station House No. 29 *(above)*. The station tower appears in the right background.

A matching view of this setting as it appears today *(below)*. The tower has long since been removed.

Charlie plays a tailor's assistant whose boss, Eric Campbell, attends a gala party using an invitation (the Count's) that Eric removes while tailoring the Count's clothes. Charlie happens upon the same party, and the two uninvited guests wreak havoc when the real Count arrives unexpectedly.

Eric sends Charlie on his way *(right)* in front of J. Dronjensky Ladies Tailor, a real shop once located at 6238 Santa Monica Boulevard in Hollywood, just east of Vine. The shop was run by Jacob Dronjensky and Max Eisman. At the time, Mr. Dronjensky lived just a few blocks away at 5811 Camerford.

The once ubiquitous, 1920s-era storefront, with a central recessed doorway, hexagonal tile floors, and twin bay display windows, has been replaced by the now ubiquitous strip mall. Today, the similarly addressed All Mart boasts, in Spanish, "Discounts," "Cheap," "Gifts."

This comparable frame from *Tillie's Punctured Romance* (1914) shows Charlie and Mabel Normand departing Heywood's, a fashionable clothing store once located at 5410 Hollywood Blvd. A motel was built on this site in 1958. As with many early films, I find this scene endearing because you can see a crowd of curious onlookers reflected in the window.

The Rink

Released December 4, 1916

Charlie plays a waiter who calculates the tab by examining the food morsels spilled on his customer's clothing. Edna invites Charlie to her skating party, where he demonstrates remarkable grace on wheels. The party soon turns into a disaster, and an angry mob chases Charlie. Still on skates, Charlie escapes by hooking his cane onto a passing car, towing him away.

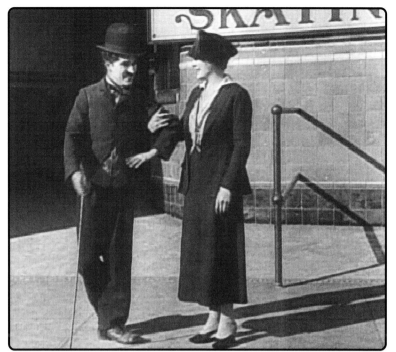

Charlie greets Edna in front of a building bearing what appears to be a large prop skating rink sign. I was not able to locate this spot, but it appears to be identical to the movie theater location employed in two Keystone films: *A Movie Star*, the 1916 lampoon of movie celebrity starring Mack Swain *(lower center)*; and Chaplin's own 1914 Keystone short, *Those Love Pangs (lower right)*. This theater may likely appear in other Keystone films. Marie Dressler's name appears on the movie poster—presumably an advertisement for Chaplin's co-starring appearance in *Tillie's Punctured Romance*—in the lower central frame.

Charlie and Edna literally meet on the street to make an appointment. The Bryson appears above Edna.

This scene was filmed in front of 678 Wilshire Place looking east down Ingraham (now Sunset Place), a bit south of Wilshire Boulevard. The home was owned by the prominent William Henry Cline family. Mr. Cline arrived in California with his parents in 1869 on one of the first transcontinental trains, then traveled to Southern California by overland wagon. His father-in-law, George Robinson, first arrived in Los Angeles in 1847, and purchased a large tract of land near downtown from Pio Pico, the last Mexican governor of California.

Paul Ayers noticed the distinctive window patterns of the building in the background of the movie frame, and correctly surmised it was the Bryson Apartments (center, above), located at 2701 Wilshire Boulevard. Built in 1913, it appears as a setting in Raymond Chandler's Philip Marlowe detective classic The Lady in the Lake, and is today a Los Angeles Historic Cultural Landmark.

This '40s era view (upper right) looks east down Wilshire past the Town House (left) towards Lafayette Park, the Bryson (arrow), and the neighboring Arcady Apartments. Built in 1927, the Arcady did not appear in the movie scene. Chaplin later filmed a scene from City Lights at the corner of the Town House.

Today, sixties-era commercial buildings (lower left) have replaced the stately homes.

This modern view (lower right) shows the Bryson from the same orientation as in the film.

Still wearing his skates, and chased by an angry mob, Charlie latches his cane onto the back of a passing car that whisks him away *(above)*. Notice how the street contains trolley tracks, and curves to the north through a small gap in the hills. The flat hill in the background is Micheltorena Hill. The corner visible in the far right background of the first frame is Silver Lake Boulevard.

The same view today *(upper right)* looking west down Sunset Boulevard from near Occidental Boulevard, towards the intersection of Silver Lake Boulevard. Paul Ayers discovered this spot.

Looking east down Sunset, Eric Campbell chases after Charlie *(lower left)*. Notice the mass of cars waiting directly behind Eric, apparently held back to accommodate the filming. In the upper right corner of the frame *(rectangle)*, you can see a narrow extension road off of Sunset that today is called Coronado Terrace. Atop a small hill, this L-shaped road runs north towards Sunset, then turns sharply west parallel to Sunset *(see west view, inset, right)*. This matching view *(lower right)* today looks east down Sunset towards Coronado Terrace in the far right background.

Inspired to go straight by a beautiful rescue mission worker (Edna), Charlie finds work as a policeman assigned to the toughest precinct in town. The film's "T" intersection set, and its depictions of poverty, spousal abuse, and drug addiction, are said to be reminiscent of Chaplin's boyhood spent on London's seedier streets. The film's highlight comes when a towering bully (Eric Campbell), intent on terrorizing Charlie by bending a gas street lamp over as a show of strength, is vanquished by gas fumes when Charlie clamps the lantern over his head.

Chaplin's tenement set presages a similar set Buster Keaton would construct on the same spot for his 1920 tenement film *Neighbors (below)*, and evokes Chaplin's boyhood London neighborhood in Lambeth. The "T" intersection pictured to the lower right looks south down Methley Street, Lambeth, London, towards No. 39, where Chaplin lived as a young boy with his mother Hannah.

This aerial photo was taken while Buster Keaton was filming *Neighbors* a few years after Chaplin had used the former Lone Star Studio. The inset shows the placement of Keaton's tenement set within the corner of the studio lot *(ellipse)* at the northeast corner of Cahuenga and Romaine. Given that this was the only corner of the studio available for constructing large sets, Chaplin must have built his similarly configured set for *Easy Street* on the same spot.

Today, a nondescript building sits on the corner of Cahuenga and Romaine *(lower right)*.

Eric chases Charlie down the set, and then around the corner from the south on Los Angeles Street, to the west on Marchessault (arrow). In the background you can see the L.A. City Water Co. plant, located on Marchessault and Alameda Street. The far structures, visible left of center, were located on Apablasa, part of the old Chinatown east of Alameda street, where Chaplin had earlier filmed scenes from *Caught in a Cabaret*.

Marchessault was named for a French pioneer who was one of the city's first non-Mexican mayors. He engineered the delivery of water from the Los Angeles River to the plaza in hollow wooden logs or zanjas. Mortified over the system's continuing failures and the resulting public outcry, Marchessault killed himself in 1869.

'The bystanders watching Charlie in the above frame are standing on the porch of this low-rise adobe that was originally the home of Augustine Olvera, for whom the adjacent alley, now a popular tourist attraction, was named. The curved arrow marks Charlie's path. The adobe was razed in 1917, and is today the site of the Biscailuz Building. The building with the stepped façade (arrow) was the Los Angeles Railway Substation, built in 1903–1904, that powered the city's many trolley lines. The front of the substation building appears in Keaton's *The Goat* (1921) discussed in two pages.

As the municipal water authority grew into larger quarters, the original water building was taken over by Chinese merchant F. See On as a curio shop. This circa-1890 photo shows the same corner view.

The Water Company building, and the historic two-story Lugo Adobe facing the plaza (far right), both survived until 1951, when, despite public outcry, they were demolished in order to provide a more sweeping vista of the Union Train Station from the plaza. Built in the 1840s by Don Vincent Lugo, the building was one of the first two-story adobes in Los Angeles. Lugo donated the adobe to St. Vincent's School, the predecessor of Loyola University. For a time it was even headquarters to Chinatown's most powerful tong, the Hop Sing. Chaplin's second wife, Lita Grey, claimed to be a descendant of the Lugo family.

This modern view *(left)* re-creates the movie frame *(far left)*. The Union Train Station tower appears in the background. The Olvera adobe on the corner has been replaced by the Biscailuz Building, home of the Mexican Cultural Institute, named for Eugene Biscailuz, a former Los Angeles city sheriff. This matching view *(below)* was taken in 1919.

This vintage photo *(below)* shows the view Chaplin would have seen as he rounded the corner onto the plaza. The F.W. Braun (later Brunswig) Drug Company building (1888) to the left appears in *Police* and *A Dog's Life*. The Plaza Church, dating from 1818, stands in the center. Its front door was used as the symbolic center of town when the city streets were first mapped. Further right, the square clock tower on Fort Moore Hill was part of Los Angeles High School, while the hilltop house to the far right is the Banning Mansion, owned by the widow of Phineas Banning, who founded Wilmington.

Felipe de Neve, with a small band of settlers, founded Los Angeles on September 4, 1781. Legend has it that when they arrived at the plaza site De Neve stuck his sword in the ground proclaiming "There you are. Do your best." From that day forward the plaza has been the symbolic heart of the city. A formal plaza was first built in 1825–1830, and stands now as the center-piece of the El Pueblo de Los Angeles Historical Monument.

De Neve laid out the early streets on a bias, instead of the true north, south, east, and west compass points, so that no street would be swept by the wind. Among the early street names were Calle Principal (Main Street), Calle Primavera (Spring Street), Calle Loma (Hill Street), Calle Aceituna (Olive Street), Calle de Las Esperanzas (Hope Street), and Calle de Las Flores (Flower Street). One street name that did not survive was Calle de Las Chulpes (Grasshopper Street).

This reverse angle shot *(above)* looks south down Los Angeles Street towards the plaza, past the narrow-angled corner of Alameda Street, running southwest to the left. The squat buildings on the narrow corner were constructed for use as bordellos. The L.A. City Water Company is the first tall building to the left. The building to its right offers chickens and ducks for sale. The background arrow marks the Garnier Building described in *Police*, the curved arrow marks Chaplin's path as he rounded the corner onto the plaza, and the ellipse marks the Baker Building described in *The Kid*.

This same narrow corner appears in the Larry Semon–Stan Laurel short, *Frauds and Frenzies* (1918) *(above)*, and in the Harold Lloyd short, *From Hand to Mouth* (1920).

Buster Keaton's 1921 short, *The Goat*, features a similar view down Los Angeles Street. The Baker Building tower appears near his head, while the Los Angeles Railway Substation fills the right edge. By chance, Chaplin and Keaton each ran around exactly the same corner, only in opposite directions, and from different vantage points.

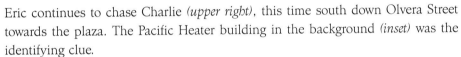

Eric continues to chase Charlie *(upper right)*, this time south down Olvera Street towards the plaza. The Pacific Heater building in the background *(inset)* was the identifying clue.

This 1920s-era photo *(upper left)* was taken before Olvera Street was converted into a tourist attraction. Charlie filmed at the far end of the street *(arrow)*.

Although stairways and landscaping block the view somewhat, this modern shot *(left)* shows the north end of Olvera Street as it appeared in the film.

This view *(right)* shows Chaplin's path *(arrow)* down Olvera Street. The porch to the left is the Avila Adobe; the oldest building in town, built in 1818. Behind it is the Los Angeles Railway Substation, which powered the city's trolleys.

This photograph shows a work crew paving Olvera Street as part of the renovation project. Chaplin would later return to this setting to film his reunion with Jackie Cooper in *The Kid (lower left)*. The ellipse in the Easy Street frame *(lower center)* matches the ellipse in the photo. A truck appears in the same position in both the photo and the lower left frame.

Originally named Wine Street, Olvera Street was renamed in honor of Judge Augustin Olvera, a signatory to the Mexican surrender to the United States in January 1847, and later the first Superior Court Judge of Los Angeles County. The street is home to the oldest building in town, the Avila Adobe, built in 1818, and the Pelanconi House, the oldest brick house in the city, dating from 1855.

In 1928, when civic leader Christine Sterling learned that the Avila Adobe was set to be demolished, she rallied a campaign to restore the building, and to convert Olvera Street into a colorful Mexican market-place and cultural center. Opening on Easter Sunday, 1930, Olvera Street remains a popular tourist destination to this day.

This 1930s view *(above)* shows Chaplin's route down Olvera Street *(arrow)* and how he earlier turned a corner onto the plaza *(curved arrow)*. The Olvera adobe that stood on that corner has been replaced by the multistory Biscailuz Building.

This aerial view of the plaza shows the relation of the two chase scene shots, and a modern view of the same setting, circa 1980.

scaped convict Charlie tunnels to the beach, popping up from the sand like a surprised gopher. After eluding the police, he swims off in a stolen bathing suit, and helps rescue a socialite family from the waves. Invited to the family's black-tie soiree, Charlie enjoys the good life until the guests discover his "Wanted" photo in the newspaper.

Bearing signs of a publicist's handiwork, Hollywood gossip columnist Grace Kingsley dutifully reported on August 11, 1917, that Chaplin rescued a 7-year-old girl from a watery grave while filming near the mouth of Topanga Canyon. Whatever else, the reported location was correct. Chaplin location enthusiast David Sameth first discovered this spot.

The beach scenes were filmed near the mouth of Topanga Canyon, shown on this 1920 map *(lower left)*.

This vintage view looking to the southeast *(lower right)* shows where Chaplin filmed at the base of Castle Rock, a former beach landmark. The large rock to the far right is called the Haystack. The site lies roughly halfway between Sunset Boulevard and Topanga Canyon Boulevard, about 300 yards south of Coastline Drive.

Charlie wrestles a shotgun away from the police, and makes his escape.

The distinctive crown-shaped rocks at the base of Castle Rock (*ellipse*) can be seen in the upper frames.

Today, most of the crown-shaped rocks have been worn away or displaced.

This 1915 view *(upper left)* looks north towards Castle Rock. The once-towering landmark was demolished on June 4, 1945 as a safety measure. The top was dynamited and leveled off as a sight-seeing promontory for motorists.

Castle Rock appeared frequently in films, not only because it was picturesque, but because until 1929, it was not possible to go much further north from this spot. The public coastline road only ran as far as Topanga Canyon before turning inland to the San Fernando Valley. The remaining coastline from Malibu north to Ventura was then private-ly owned.

May Rindge, widow of wealthy ranch owner Frederick Rindge, fought tenaciously for decades following his death in 1905 to keep their massive Malibu land holdings pri-vate. She built locked gates and hired armed guards to keep out trespassers, and even built a pri-vate rail line to preempt Southern Pacific from claiming legal rights to lay tracks across her land.

After years of legal battles, the U.S. Supreme Court affirmed the state's eminent domain rights in 1923, leading to the construction of Roosevelt Highway (today Pacific Coast Highway), which opened in June 1929. Facing financial setbacks, and weary of the fight, May Rindge was forced to sell her estate, and died impoverished in 1941.

This view today *(upper right)* shows how Castle Rock has been flattened. The arrow points to the southern side of the Haystack Rock.

Among dozens of films shot beside Castle Rock, the Keystone bathing beauties frolic in *Hearts and Flowers* (1919) *(left)*, and from *Fatty and Mabel Adrift* (1916) we see the crown-shaped rocks and Haystack Rock through the back of the porch *(center)*, and Luke the dog chase Al St. John towards the Haystack Rock *(right)*.

Chaplin's *Burlesque on Carmen* (released in two-reels on December 18, 1915, and in four-reels on April 22, 1916) was filmed in part on the beach north of Castle Rock. After Chaplin left Essanay, the studio expanded the film without his authority by inserting outtakes and footage with new actors. Outraged, Chaplin unsuccessfully sued to enjoin the studio from tampering with his work.

A band of smugglers land their boat during the opening of the film. The unique profile of the Haystack Rock appears in the background.

Chaplin's counterpart to Carmen's Don Jose appears as "Darn Hosiery."

Although the foreground rocks now appear to be submerged in the sand, the distinctive profile of Haystack Rock matches the movie frames.

Charlie flees the police by speeding down a steep dirt road. In the background, a far distant ridgeline *(ellipse)* protrudes above the near ridgeline.

This aerial view shows *(arrow)* how Charlie ran onto Pacific Coast Highway. The large mansion in the center is the Leon Villa, located beneath, and often mistaken for, the Getty Villa, the original branch of the J. Paul Getty Museum.

This shot was likely filmed looking north where Coastline Drive joins Pacific Coast Highway. David Totheroh, grandson of Chaplin's principal cameraman Rollie Totheroh, spotted the same distinctive, distant ridgeline *(ellipse)* confirming the location.

Charlie scampers away from the police. This frame, and the vintage view to the right, both show how undeveloped the coastal highway was during the time of filming.

This view shows the newly opened Roosevelt Highway wending its way north past Castle Rock. The Leon Villa *(ellipse)* stands watch.

The same view of the wider and straighter Pacific Coast Highway today.

Charlie poses with the Haystack Rock in the background.

The same view today, taken by David Totheroh.

This aerial view shows the Haystack Rock (*circle*) and what remains of Castle Rock (*square*), in the shadow of the Leon Villa to the left. The 35-room mansion was built in 1927 at a cost of $1 million by textile merchant Leon Kauffman, who made his fortune in the wool market during World War I. Kauffman and his wife died in the early 1930s, and for 17 years the home sat vacant until it sold at auction for a mere $71,000.

The action switches from an isolated beach to a seaside resort. These scenes were all filmed on the Center Street Pier looking north to the Abbott Kinney Pier in Venice (Center Street is now named North Venice Boulevard). The Big Dipper roller coaster running along the pier (*left*) was built in May 1920 after Chaplin filmed here in 1917. The pier was completely destroyed by a fire on December 20, 1920 (*see* By the Sea *chapter*). Rebuilt in 1921, the pier also appears in *The Circus*.

The tower of the Venice Auditorium appears in the background.

The Ferris wheel and the crow's nest of the Ship Cafe appear by Edna's head.

The Venice Dance Hall appears between Eric Campbell and Henry Bergman.

This aerial view of the pier was taken before the Big Dipper roller coaster was built. Through the magic of film editing, Charlie dumps Eric into the water at the Abbott Kinney Pier *(lower middle)*, yet retrieves him from the water at the Center Street Pier *(lower left)*. The arrow in the lower left frame shows from where on the Abbott Kinney Pier Eric takes the plunge.

Eric's spill into the water *(lower center)* was filmed beside the Captive Aeroplane ride, a rotating tower from which airplane-shaped carts swung on chains over the water. You can see the resting airplanes in the background, along with most of the west side of the Venice Auditorium, and the "MUIRAUQA" sign *(see reverse insert)* for the Venice Aquarium situated just west of the auditorium. The lower right photo shows the airplane tower and auditorium from a similar view as the movie frame. Notice the Ferris wheel to the far right.

Chaplin's favorite lead villain, 37-year-old Scotsman Eric Campbell, had appeared in each of Chaplin's Mutual films, excluding Chaplin's solo film *One A.M.* Tragically, Campbell died in an early morning auto accident after completing *The Adventurer*. Chaplin's subsequent films would lack the special comic menace Campbell brought to the screen.

This view (left) looks east down the Abbott Kinney Pier from the Ferris wheel towards the Ship Cafe, a landmark restaurant popular with the Hollywood crowd, constructed in the shape of a large sailing ship. Here the Ship Cafe points perpendicular to the shore. When the pier was rebuilt in 1921 after a disastrous fire, the Ship Cafe was rebuilt to face parallel to the shore. You can see the Ferris wheel and the crow's nest of the Ship Cafe beside Eric Campbell's head (right).

During a chase from Harold Lloyd's 1920 short *Number Please?*, Harold dashes south at the far west end of the pier towards the Captive Aeroplane ride tower (left). The circular building to his right was a brightly colored Sunkist orange juice stand. The railing in the background is near where Chaplin stood when he dumped Eric Campbell into the water.

Continuing Harold's chase (right), you can see, starting from left to right, the Ship Cafe, the Ferris wheel, and the Captive Aeroplane tower. If you were to stroll west down the pier from the Ferris wheel you would pass a large skating rink to your left, then the Venice Auditorium to your right, and finally the Venice Aquarium further down on your right. At the end of the pier was an amusement ride called Over the Falls.

Earlier in the film, Charlie rescues Edna and her mother from the water. These scenes were obviously filmed safely within some indoor swimming pool, as you can see windows of light reflected in the water. Although this scene could have been filmed at other public pools close by, since the Venice Plunge was located right at the Abbott Kinney Pier filming location, and Chaplin had previously filmed the exterior of the plunge in *By the Sea*, there is a good chance this is where Chaplin filmed these water scenes. The view (*right*) shows the interior of the Venice Plunge. The rectangle below shows the Venice Plunge just north of the Abbott Kinney Pier.

This reverse angle view shows again where Harold Lloyd (*above left*) ran towards the Captive Aeroplane tower (*left star*), and where Chaplin stood (*right star*). The ellipse shows the "MUIRAUQA" sign visible in the Chaplin (*above center*) frame. This far end of the pier is extensively reconfigured from how it appeared in 1914 at the conclusion of *Tillie's Punctured Romance*.

The Chaplin Studio

As Chaplin's Mutual contract wound down in 1917, the First National Corporation offered him an independent production deal in exchange for distribution rights. First National not only outbid Mutual, but offered Chaplin complete creative control, ownership rights to his films, and a chance to build his own studio. Construction of the studio started in November 1917, and by January 21, 1918, Chaplin had planted his footprints and signature into a cement walkway, signaling the studio's completion. The First National contract called for Chaplin to create eight two-reel comedies within a span of 16 months. Instead, it would take Chaplin nearly five years to satisfy the contract.

Chaplin completed his last movie shot at the studio, *Limelight*, in 1952. When traveling abroad for the movie's London premiere, Chaplin, who had never obtained U.S. citizenship, was told his re-entry permit to the United States would be denied. Chaplin thus moved to Switzerland, where he would live the rest of his life, and arranged to liquidate his American holdings. Chaplin sold the studio in 1953, and it has since been variously owned by comedian Red Skelton, CBS, and A&M Records, home of Herb Alpert's Tijuana Brass. The studio stands at 1416 North La Brea in Hollywood, and is now owned by the Jim Henson Company.

Chaplin built his studio on a lemon orchard located within the northwest corner of La Brea and De Longpre in Hollywood, just south of Sunset Boulevard. The north end of the property contained a mansion that Syd Chaplin, Chaplin's brother and business manager, would occupy. Chaplin documented the construction of his studio with a playful documentary, *How to Make Movies* (1918), that he had hoped would count for one of the eight films he owed to First National. First National politely declined, and before the advent of DVDs, the film was not widely distributed. Most of the vintage studio images presented in this chapter come from this film.

This panorama of the studio, looking up La Brea to the left, and down De Longpre to the right, was created from a shot of Charlie driving to work. Chaplin's office was situated on the corner, and could be accessed privately through a back door, sheltered by a small porch. The corner office has a prominent brick chimney, corresponding to the interior fireplace mantle where Chaplin would display his first Oscar. The trusses for the open-air filming stage appear to the right. The studio's delightful English cottage exterior helped to appease local residents who had objected to the studio being built.

As if by magic, the studio springs into form during this time-lapse sequence taken from *How to Make Movies*.

This panorama shot looks eastward across the Chaplin Studio's open-air stage.

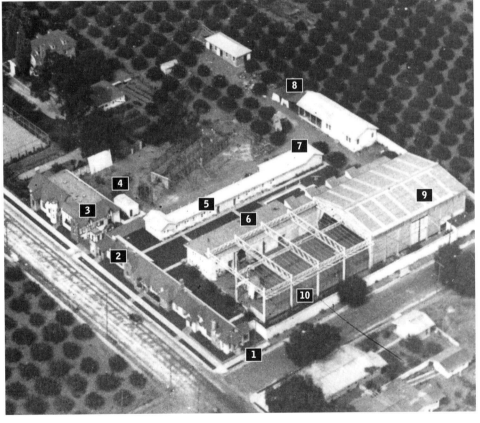

This aerial photo appears to have been taken during the production of *Pay Day* in 1921. Starting clockwise from the bottom corner, the stars indicate: 1) Chaplin's office, 2) the screening room, 3) the film laboratory, 4) the concrete film storage vault, 5) the long low row of dressing rooms, 6) the cement walkway adjacent to the studio pool, where Chaplin left his footprints, 7) the studio garage, 8) the carpenter shop, 9) the closed shooting stage, and 10) the open-air stage adjacent to Chaplin's office.

This studio map may date from 1925, as Chaplin's photo appears to come from *The Gold Rush* released that year.

This aerial view *(and detail, middle)* was taken during the production of *The Circus* (1926–1927). Notice the half circus tent set. Hollywood's narrow streets were adequate for orchards and bungalows, but in 1929 La Brea and other urban streets were widened. This detail of the north gate *(far right)* shows how it once projected out from the laboratory building. To accommodate the wider street, the decorative gables and bay windows of the studio north of the main gate were chopped flush to meet the sidewalk *(middle right)*.

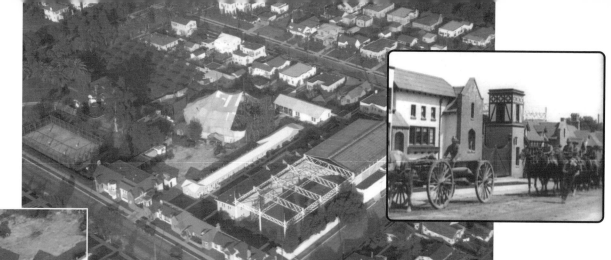

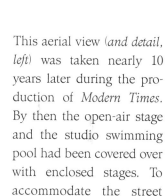

This aerial view *(and detail, left)* was taken nearly 10 years later during the production of *Modern Times*. By then the open-air stage and the studio swimming pool had been covered over with enclosed stages. To accommodate the street widening, the studio wing south of the main gate was relocated eastward several feet in order to preserve its quaint details. The resulting move placed Chaplin's corner office almost squarely against the closed corner stage. The north gate *(right middle)* now sits flush with the rest of the laboratory building.

We now begin a clockwise tour of the studio, discussing the landmarks depicted in the aerial photograph. We begin with Chaplin's office. Standing on the fireplace mantle (insert) appears to be Chaplin's first Oscar, awarded May 16, 1929, "for versatility and genius in writing, acting, directing and producing *The Circus*." The initial Academy of Motion Picture Arts and Sciences Awards were bestowed in 1929 for works created during 1927–1928. Chaplin was presented with a Special Award.

A view of Chaplin's former office as it appears today.

Looking east, this contemporary view shows Chaplin's former corner office.

Looking south, this view from inside the studio shows the walkway towards Chaplin's former office.

Looking north, secretary Nelly Bly Baker brings an armload of mail towards Chaplin's office. The ellipse at her feet marks her location on the images *(left and below)*.

This composite image also looks north. The rectangle marks the corner of the studio screening room. The circle at the upper right marks the corner of the studio laboratory building, north of the entrance gate. These elements appear in the modern images below.

This modern view looks north from Chaplin's office. The ellipse matches the frames above.

Moving a bit further north, this modern view shows the same corner of the screening room *(rectangle)* and the corner of the laboratory building *(circle)* pictured above. The square marks the studio vault door.

This view shows Chaplin walking west towards the screening room. The studio gate entrance is to his right. The building with three windows was part of the ladies' dressing room wing.

The same view today. The ladies' dressing room wing has been removed.

Chaplin entertains a visit from Winston Churchill in 1929 during the filming of *City Lights*. They are pictured leaving the studio screening room. The studio entrance gate is behind them.

Inside the screening room projection booth. Many electrical circuits and switches appear to be original.

Built in 1918, the studio screening room is still used for that purpose today.

Just north of the screening room stands the main entrance gate to the studio. The laboratory building pictured to the left originally had two southward-facing dormer windows, but lost one dormer after the adjacent street was widened. To the far right is one of the doors to the studio vault.

Originally built as a small concrete bunker, the studio film vault *(below)* still stands in place, but has been incorporated into a newer two-story office building. The southern-facing vault door pictured here opens to the outside. The other vault door, facing east, opens into the building's interior reception area. Where Chaplin once stored priceless reels of exposed film, the vault now safeguards office supplies.

Chaplin's straight-faced valet, Tom Harrington, retrieves Chaplin's most treasured possession, a pair of the Little Tramp's boots.

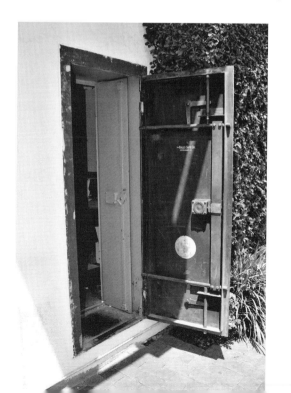

The gothic window of the editing room appears to the north side of the studio gate. The editing room once projected out closer to the sidewalk from the rest of the building. When La Brea was widened, the editing room was pushed back flush with the rest of the building.

Chaplin studies a strip of film in the studio editing room. In the background, a car driving south down La Brea *(arrow)* appears through the gothic window. The windows to the left look down onto the studio entrance.

The Chaplin Studio had its own film developing laboratory.

The side windows of the editing room *(oval)* overlook the studio entrance gate.

This view looks west towards the studio entrance. From left to right we see the protruding wing of the ladies' dressing room, the studio tower south of the entrance, the twin southern-facing dormer windows of the studio laboratory, and in the foreground, the low-rising studio vault. The southern-facing vault door is open *(between the two women)* while the second vault door, facing the camera *(far right)* is closed.

The western view towards the studio gate today.

This view of the entrance gate comes from a 16mm home movie taken in 1940 by Syd Chaplin. Notice above the right side of the gate that there is now only one southern facing dormer window.

As an affectionate tribute to the studio's heritage, a figure of Kermit the Frog, wearing a tramp costume, stands atop the studio gate tower.

The rectangle marks the portion of the dressing room wing that has been removed. The screening room door in the background is open.

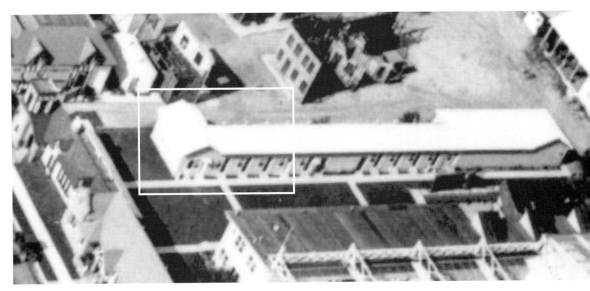

This modern view looks towards the screening room. The rectangle suggests the portion of the ladies' dressing rooms that have been removed. The women's restroom door (designated with a Miss Piggy sign) was originally the opening to a narrow breezeway leading through the dressing room wing, and to an interior women's restroom door. The studio restrooms remain in their original location.

This aerial detail shows the portion of the dressing room wing (*rectangle*) that was removed some time after 1955. (The wing was still intact in the studio's 1955 Sanborn fire insurance map.) To the immediate right of the rectangle are the twin breezeway openings between which were located the studio restrooms. The men's section of dressing rooms commence with the windows and doors further right. The far right end of the wing, with no windows, is the back of the studio garage.

Chaplin and visiting Scottish comedian Harry Lauder walk beside the twin breezeway openings. While these openings once lead to interior restroom doors, today they serve as exterior entrances to the studio restrooms.

A bevy of bathing beauties walk past the men's dressing rooms towards the back of the garage.

The actors and crew enjoy a dip in the studio pool. The peaked roof of the studio garage (circle) appears in the contemporary photo (below left).

The narrow walkway past the men's dressing rooms leading to the garage (ellipse) as it appears today. To the immediate right is the edge of the small stage built over the studio pool sometime before 1936.

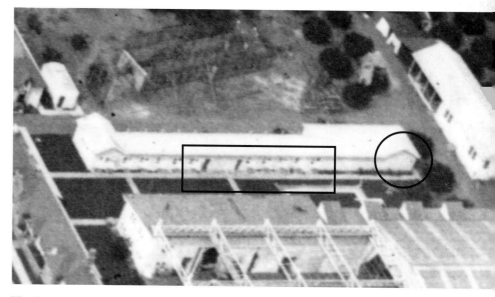

The long rectangle in this aerial shot marks the twin breezeway openings (upper left) and men's dressing rooms (upper middle), while the circle marks the back of the garage (upper right).

Chaplin entertains visiting First National exhibitors on the central lawn between the dressing room wing to the left, and the closed stage to the right. The pool is behind them. The rectangle in each image marks the easternmost of two wide breezeways passing south from the central lawn to the stages. At the very center, young Jackie Coogan sits astride Chaplin's shoulders, while Chaplin's future second wife, Lita Grey, sits coiled at his feet. Chaplin staged this event to appease the distributors, who had been expecting a steady stream of short films while Charlie was lavishing time and energy producing his first feature-length film, *The Kid*.

Charlie enjoys boxing on the studio central lawn. Behind him, two sidewalks cut across the lawn from the dressing rooms on the left to the stage on the right. The near sidewalk has since been removed, but the far sidewalk, passing to the easternmost breezeway of the stage *(square)* is still in place. This far sidewalk contains Chaplin's footprints.

The same view looking east today, showing the truncated dressing room wing *(left)* and the small Stage Three that sits on the site of the former pool. The east stage breezeway *(rectangle)* remains unchanged.

Chaplin's signature and footprints set into the studio path on January 21, 1918.

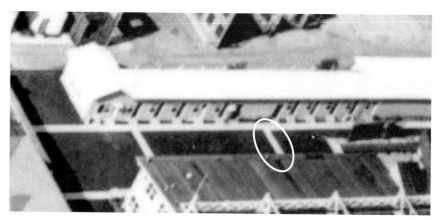

The ellipse in this aerial view shows part of the pathway containing Chaplin's footprints.

A few shallow imprints *(ellipses)* still appear in the cement. It is reported that the sidewalk block containing Chaplin's signature was removed to Red Skelton's home during the time Skelton owned the studio from between 1958 to 1962.

Paul Ayers, the author, and Jeffrey Castel de Oro sit on the Stage Three steps. This recording studio has been used by recording artists such as Bruce Springsteen and the Rolling Stones. In 1985, dozens of artists gathered here to record the *We Are the World* fundraising album. The ellipse on the walk marks Chaplin's nearly 90-year-old footprints. The door on the back wall is the men's room door, identified with a Kermit sign.

These frames show Chaplin inspecting a lemon tree on the studio grounds, the open porch of the studio carpenter shop, and the corresponding views today.

The arrows in this aerial view show the direction and placement of the camera recording the movie frames *(above left)*. The lemon tree stood between the east end of the dressing room wing and the carpenter shop *(bottom arrow)*. The open-air carpenter shop porch appears a bit further north *(top arrow)*.

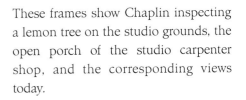

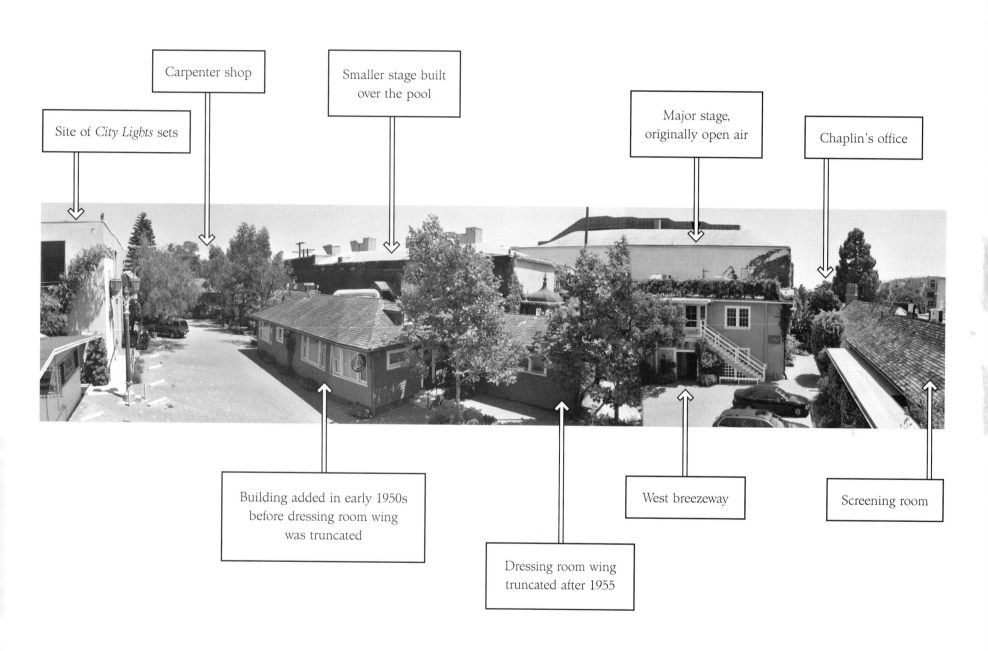

Site of *City Lights* sets

Carpenter shop

Smaller stage built over the pool

Major stage, originally open air

Chaplin's office

Building added in early 1950s before dressing room wing was truncated

Dressing room wing truncated after 1955

West breezeway

Screening room

This panoramic view looks east to south, taken from the balcony of the office building standing over the studio vault.

Reminiscent of *The Champion*, Charlie once again teams up with a lovable dog, this time a mongrel named Scraps. Outcasts Charlie and Scraps befriend Edna, who sings for tips in a seedy cabaret. After Scraps uncovers some thieves' buried cash, and the crooks are properly arrested, Charlie and Edna purchase an idyllic farm.

The film closes as the couple gaze happily into a cradle, revealed to contain Scraps and a litter of puppies. The slum set *(left)* was built at Chaplin's newly constructed studio.

The film opens with this grim urban view *(upper right)*, filmed looking east down Republic Street, past the Brunswig Drug Company building *(center)*, towards the Pico House *(arrow)* and the Merced Theater to its right, on Main Street, just south of the plaza.

The Pico House hotel, still standing on the corner of Main and the plaza, was built in 1869 by Don Pio Pico, the last Mexican governor of Alta California before it was surrendered to the United States in 1847. The Pico House was the city's first three-story masonry building, and the first hotel to offer bathtubs with running water. The Banning stagecoaches running from the port at Wilmington would stop at the Pico House, and the first street car line in Los Angeles also had its terminus at the hotel, running south down Main Street. Also still standing, the Merced Theater was the city's first indoor stage. It opened New Year's Day 1870, with programs in English and Spanish.

Republic Street was a very short east-west passage from New High Street to Main Street. The details of the Pico House windows appear at the end of the block.

A similar view taken from New High Street today. The ellipse matches the former corner where Harold Lloyd stood *(middle right)* for a scene from *Hand to Mouth* (1920).

Another view of the same corner from *Hand to Mouth (left)*, this time looking north up New High Street as it passes the corner of Republic. The building on the near corner has been demolished for a parking lot. This view also appears in Chaplin's earlier film, *Police*.

The ellipse marks the same spot in movie frame *(left)*, the present-day photo of the Brunswig Building *(above)* and in this vintage aerial view *(lower right)*. The cupola towers of the Baker Building *(see* The Kid*)* appear in the lower right corner of the aerial shot.

The Brunswig Building as it looked from Main Street. The building still stands.

By 1918, Chaplin had become so popular that unauthorized copies of his films were commonly circulated. To combat this practice, Chaplin began authenticating his films by personally signing the title cards *(right)*.

Shoulder Arms originally featured domestic scenes of Charlie at home with his children and domineering wife before leaving for The Great War in France. The theatrical release begins with Charlie already in boot camp. Once at the front, Charlie rescues a fellow soldier behind enemy lines, and later befriends a beautiful French girl (Edna). Impersonating a German officer, Charlie ends up capturing the Kaiser, and returns to camp a triumphant hero. Alas, Charlie awakens to find that his adventures were only a dream.

Although some critics feared Chaplin would trivialize the war, while others grumbled that, despite his efforts selling war bonds, Chaplin did not actually enlist for military service, *Shoulder Arms* proved to be a tremendous success. Released a month before the armistice ending World War I, America relished the chance to laugh away the painful times.

This marvelous production still, looking east, shows Chaplin at work in Venice at the southeast corner of Market Street and Ocean Front Walk. Chaplin and three young actors are filming an early domestic scene that was cut from the final release of the film. The young boy watching the filming *(arrow)* is Jack Totheroh, son of Chaplin's cameraman Rollie Totheroh. Jack is also pictured, at age 90, in the chapter for *The Gold Rush*. The woman peeking out directly above Jack is his mother Ida. The man shading the camera above Jack may be Rollie himself. Spanning the history of cinema, Jack played an infant in the 1915 Niles, Essanay film *The Bachelor's Baby*, and a cameraman role in Richard Attenborough's 1992 biopic *Chaplin*.

Charlie and his sons walk west down Market Street. Moments later Charlie dashes quickly into the bar, and returns presumably refreshed before continuing his family stroll.

So much has been demolished and remodeled that this modern view *(below)* barely compares to the original view *(upper, left)*.

The Hotel Rose is marked with a rectangle in both of these vintage views. The arrow *(left)* points to the site where the photo was taken. The curved roof of the Venice Plunge stands between the shooting site and the beach.

Charlie and sons continue their stroll south down La Brea alongside Chaplin's corner office at the Chaplin Studio.

The same view today. The steps leading to the side door on La Brea have been removed.

This view of Chaplin's corner office shows the film site (above).

 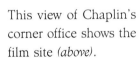

This view of Chaplin marching may have been filmed looking north up Fairfax towards Wilshire in the background. Oil derricks seem to appear in the left background. A plane from Syd Chaplin's fleet (inset).

This shot from near the end of the film also appears to have been filmed at a similar setting. Oil derricks seem to appear in the right background.

Charlie and company in formation.

David Totheroh reports that his grandfather Rollie clearly remembered filming scenes for *Shoulder Arms* at what would become Syd Chaplin's Airfield (which later became Roger's Airport) at the southwest corner of Wilshire Blvd. and Fairfax Avenue. The Syd Chaplin Aircraft Corporation, founded in 1919 by Charlie's brother, established the first regular air service from Los Angeles to Catalina Island using a Curtis "Seagull" flying boat. Famed director Cecil B. DeMille, one of Hollywood's aviation pioneers, founded the Mercury Aviation Company located at DeMille's own airfield across the street.

This view *(lower right)* looks up Fairfax at the intersection with Wilshire. The newly constructed hangers of the Chaplin airfield line the left edge of the street. The DeMille field is to the middle left. Based on the angles of the streets and other details, the lowest ellipse suggests where Chaplin could have filmed the marching scene *(upper left)*. The left oval marks the future site of the Farmer's Market, which opened in 1934 at 3rd and Fairfax, while the right oval marks the La Brea Tar Pits on Wilshire near Fairfax, where Ice Age fossils were first discovered in 1905.

Stuck in a trench, Charlie reminisces of home. The city portion of this split screen image was filmed looking south from atop the Hill Street Tunnel towards 1st Street. One telling clue: the Hotel La Crosse situated at 122 South Hill Street, appears in each of these images. The distance above the tunnel created the illusion of great height when looking down the street.

The top of the Hill Street Tunnel, facing south, appears in the Harold Lloyd short film, *Never Weaken* (1921).

This setting appears again *(left)* in Harold Lloyd's short, *High and Dizzy* (1920), while Larry Semon *(inset)* dangles from telephone wires in *The Sleuth* (1922).

Buster Keaton also filmed a high-rise scene here *(right)* for his first feature film, *Three Ages* (1923). Notice how the trolley tracks swerve to the right in order to line up with the northern bore of the twin tunnel.

The arrow *(left)* in this circa-1925 view marks the distinctive twin bores of the Hill Street Tunnel. The circle marks the Bradbury mansion a half-block away where Chaplin filmed *Work* in 1915. The soaring L.A. City Hall tower would be built a few years later at the right-edge center of this photo.

Situated at the dead end of a short and inaccessible street, the top of the Hill Street Tunnel was an exceptionally popular place to film. It was easy to build large sets here without disrupting traffic, while its remote location assured minimal crowds of onlookers. Interestingly, Chaplin only used the setting for a mundane shot.

This detail looks at the south face of the Hill Street Tunnel.

This production still from the 1921 Universal serial *The Terror Trail* reveals how the position of the buildings down the street create the illusion that the set is high off of the ground.

Wearing a humorous tree costume, Charlie infiltrates enemy lines and rescues a fellow doughboy played by his brother Syd. Apparently, Chaplin filmed these scenes during a sweltering August heat wave.

The Robinson biography reports that some outdoor sequences were filmed in Sherman, an early community nestled near the foothills of Beverly Hills. Paul Ayers

helped determine that this view *(right)* likely looks south towards the long windbreak of eucalyptus trees running along Wilshire Boulevard *(horizontal arrow)* and intersecting with Doheny Avenue *(diagonal arrow)*. The Baldwin Hills appear faintly in the background.

Looking north towards the likely filming area *(ellipse)* in relation to Doheny *(white arrow)* and the long windbreak running along Wilshire Boulevard *(black arrow)*. Starting from Santa Monica Boulevard, this prominent row of trees ran east past Doheny all the way to Robertson.

Another view *(far left)* looking south a bit further up into the hills. The same stretch of Wilshire and Doheny can be seen through the trees.

This contemporary view, taken by Paul Ayers near a hill above North Doheny Drive and St. Ives in West Hollywood, compares to the same view *(upper right)*. Wilshire and Doheny are now buried from view by many buildings and trees.

Chased by a German soldier, Charlie dashes for the concealing safety of a windbreak. Once among the trees, Charlie escapes his pursuer.

This 1920 aerial view looks north towards Beverly Hills. The Beverly Hills Hotel (*ellipse*) appears in the far distance. Wilshire Boulevard (*diagonal arrow*) and a section of the long windbreak running parallel to the street appear at the bottom. The right arrow marks Santa Monica Boulevard.

The Robinson biography reports that Chaplin filmed the forest scenes along Wilshire Boulevard. While it is not possible to identify any precise spot, it seems likely that Chaplin filmed within the Wilshire windbreak of eucalyptus trees, a section of which appears here, as the trees in this forest scene (*left*) are clearly eucalyptus. The background road (presumably Wilshire) must have been fairly well-traveled, as you can see several cars pass by (*arrow*) during the brief scene.

This stunning photo shows the "gas bags" in formation at the U.S. Army Balloon School in Arcadia. A newspaper account reports Chaplin filmed scenes out at the school on August 31, 1918, a few weeks before the film premiered. The school was located on 200 acres of the historic Baldwin Ranch, at what would later become Ross Field, and is now the site of the Santa Anita Park racetrack. Construction of the military school began in June 1918, and was completed a few weeks before the WWI armistice. Four thousand men were stationed here to be trained in the handling of observation, captive, and dirigible balloons. For a number of reasons, I believe that these hero's welcome scenes *(left)* concluding the film were likely shot at the school.

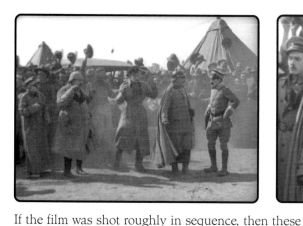

If the film was shot roughly in sequence, then these hero's welcome scenes, among the final scenes of the movie, would have likely been filmed in late August or early September, corresponding to the August 31 press account. Next, unlike the early camp scenes where Chaplin performs with a small group of "soldiers" recognizable as Chaplin Studio actors, the hero's welcome scene here includes dozens of enthusiastic soldiers. The easiest way to obtain a large number of cooperative military extras would be to visit a military base or school such as the Balloon School.

Also, since Chaplin filmed all of his other outdoor scenes very close to his studio, it would have made little sense for him to travel all the way east out to Arcadia unless he had a special purpose. Lastly, during the welcome scene you can see some very tall, steep-pitched tents in the background, noticeably different from the small pup tents used in the early camp scenes. Similar tall, steep-pitched tents appear in this photo of the Balloon School.

Thus, while speculation, it makes perfect sense that Chaplin traveled to Arcadia to film the hero's welcome scene—not because of its location, but to gain access to the readily available soldiers there to serve as extras.

Sunnyside

Released June 15, 1919

Charlie plays an all-purpose hotel desk clerk, cook, janitor, handyman, and cattle herder in the pastoral town of Sunnyside. In one famous scene, Charlie dreams of himself dancing in a glade with four wood nymphs.

Looking to the southeast, Charlie rides a farm cart along this dirt lane.

Charlie strolls south through the village set towards a church. As discussed in *A Day's Pleasure*, the church tower appears in the back of the Bullock's Department Store set used in that film.

Paul Ayers surmised that this scene was filmed looking south from the Burbank side of the Hollywood hills, and found this matching ridgeline shot at the intersection of California and Alameda in Burbank, facing almost due south. A number of original streams nearby, which feed out of the Tujunga Wash into the Los Angeles River, likely provided the setting for all of the rustic scenes from the movie. The location is close to the Burbank NBC studios at Alameda and Olive.

A Day's Pleasure

Released December 15, 1919

Charlie, Edna, and their "sons" set out for a day's pleasure, first touring by automobile, and then taking a disastrous harbor cruise. Chaplin was lavishing so much time on his first feature-length production *The Kid* that he quickly knocked out this film to placate his impatient First National distributors.

Despite his full acquittal on trumped up manslaughter charges following the 1921 death of Virginia Rappé in San Francisco, popular comedian Roscoe "Fatty" Arbuckle, who had worked with Chaplin in 1914, was banned from appearing on screen, and turned to directing instead. This 1925 Lloyd Hamilton short, *The Movies*, directed by Arbuckle, is filled with inside jokes about the film industry. Probably few people ever caught this extreme inside joke—the hospital "set" appearing in the film is the back of Chaplin's office.

When Buster Keaton sets off for a trip with his "family" in *The Boat* (1921), the boys wear little Buster hats. The boys in Chaplin's "family" wear similar Chaplin derbies.

As Edna and the boys wait, Charlie steps from the back entrance of his studio office at the corner of La Brea and De Longpre. Jackie Coogan, the future star of *The Kid*, plays Charlie's younger son.

The same corner as it appears today.

Charlie and company embark on a pleasure cruise from the Southern Pacific Passenger Station in San Pedro *(upper left)*, located just north of where the east end of Fifth Street terminated at the water *(see "D" on map, inset)*. (Fifth Street originally ran straight and parallel to Fourth and Sixth Streets, but it has since been reconfigured.) This view of the terminal building was taken looking west across the main channel of Los Angeles Harbor from Terminal Island. The photo detail *(middle left)* shows the boat terminal appearing in the movie.

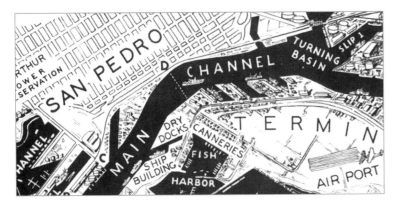

The ferry building site provided ferry service across the main channel from San Pedro to Terminal Island. A modern ferry berth *(right)* stands in place of the old passenger station.

Paul Ayers noted that as Charlie's boat departs, Dead Man's Island appears in the background *(left)*.

This photo shows Dead Man's Island, a prominent harbor landmark that has since been removed. The island apparently received its name as a burial ground for the U.S. marines who died when Mexico successfully expelled the United States' occupying forces from Los Angeles in 1846.

Dead Man's Island appears briefly in Chaplin's 1915 Essanay film, *Shanghaied*, which was also filmed near San Pedro.

This circa-1890 photo *(right)* shows the passenger station, and Dead Man's Island in the distance behind the tall ships.

Chaplin filmed aboard the pleasure boat *Ace*, leased for $5 an hour from the San Pedro Transportation Company. In the background, you can see vintage battleships and the Angel's Gate Lighthouse, built in 1913, that still stands today at the end of a 9,250-foot-long breakwater. The black musician's face is made up white to suggest that he is seasick.

These vintage images show the lighthouse and battleships in the harbor. The breakwater was built from between 1899 to 1910, using granite boulders excavated from Santa Catalina Island. The breakwater was further extended in 1928, making possible the development of Long Beach Harbor into the busiest port on the West Coast.

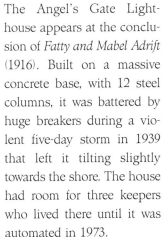

The Angel's Gate Lighthouse appears at the conclusion of *Fatty and Mabel Adrift* (1916). Built on a massive concrete base, with 12 steel columns, it was battered by huge breakers during a violent five-day storm in 1939 that left it tilting slightly towards the shore. The house had room for three keepers who lived there until it was automated in 1973.

The lighthouse still guards the harbor today. The Vincent Thomas Bridge connecting San Pedro and Terminal Island appears in the background. It was completed in 1963.

Charlie and crew stop to take orders from a traffic cop. The sign on the building corner says Bullock's, a famous department store located downtown at the northwest corner of Seventh Street and Broadway.

The real Bullock's appears in this 1920s vintage photo. At the time, it was one of the largest commercial buildings in town, and the first building to introduce escalators. It is now home to the Los Angeles Jewelry Mart.

As shown in this production still, the scene was filmed on the Chaplin Studio lot. The church tower from the *Sunnyside* set *(right)* appears in the background.

For some reason, Chaplin took the trouble to re-create an actual downtown location. The set even replicates the four-way intersecting trolley tracks that ran through the crossroads of Seventh and Broadway.

Jeffrey Vance, author of the beautiful volume *Chaplin: Genius of the Cinema*, theorizes that Chaplin had originally shot footage downtown, but frustrated at the inconvenience of filming on location, decided to finish shooting at the studio instead. Chaplin re-created the Bullock's corner in order to match the later studio shots with the earlier scenes filmed on location. However, after going to all of that trouble, it appears that none of the true location scenes appear in the film.

The Kid

Released February 6, 1921

Hoping to give her infant son a better life, struggling single mother Edna leaves her baby inside a millionaire's limousine, pinning a note to his blanket. When thieves steal the car, they abandon the baby on the street, where Charlie finds him and raises the child as his own. Five years later, Charlie and the Kid (Jackie Coogan) are partners in petty crime; Jackie patrols the neighborhood breaking windows, while Charlie repairs them for a fee.

Edna has since become a wealthy singer who helps slum children with the hope of finding her son. When orphanage officials discover Jackie is not Charlie's son, they take him away, but Charlie finds a shortcut across the slum rooftops and rescues Jackie from their truck. Edna recognizes the note the officials recover from Charlie, and realizes Jackie is her son.

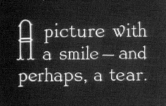

A picture with a smile — and perhaps, a tear.

The film concludes as Jackie and Charlie are reunited at Edna's stately home.

This title card (*upper middle*) introduces the film.

Chaplin lavished more than a year filming *The Kid*, his longest project to date. Although First National touted the film's six reel length (*lower left*), it had expected a series of shorter films instead.

The image of the Tramp and the Kid has become one of the great movie icons.

This establishing shot shows the Charity Hospital where Edna delivers the baby who would grow up to become the Kid. Notice the peaked gables, and the stone gate pillars.

Flipping through a Los Angeles history book, I noticed a page showing turn-of-the-century college campuses, including this photo of Occidental College (right). Somehow I recognized that the building in the foreground matched the "maternity hospital" appearing in The Kid. After quickly checking the L.A. Main Library website, I determined that the building in question was the former Occidental College Hall of Letters. The building to the far left is the former Charles M. Stimson Library.

By the time Chaplin filmed here, Occidental College had already moved to its present location in the Eagle Rock neighborhood of Los Angeles. The Sanborn fire insurance maps establish that by 1920 the "hospital" building was abandoned, explaining both its derelict appearance in the movie, and its availability for use as a set. Notice how the corner stone gate pillars in the photo are similar to the eastern gate pillars shown in the movie frame (upper left).

Her only sin being motherhood, Edna enters a hostile and uncertain world. Kevin Brownlow likens this structure to the London workhouse where the destitute Chaplins were incarcerated during Charlie's impoverished youth.

The west and east sides of the "hospital" building have identical doorways. Although Chaplin filmed at the back (east) side of the building *(presented in two pages)*, this frame blow-up shows how the east side doorway details match the west side of the building today. The "hospital" building is located at the northeast corner of North Avenue Fifty and North Figueroa Street. Today the building is centered in the middle of the block, set far back from the streets, and is hemmed in by a number of smaller homes and commercial buildings.

I don't think anyone living today in these humble apartments, or working today at the Cartique Body Shop, could possibly imagine that two United States Presidents and one of the most famous entertainers in the world had all once visited their neighborhood. The van *(box)* marks the approximate spot of the open convertibles where President Roosevelt *(upper left)* and President Taft *(upper right)* were once photographed during campus events. Edna's scene was filmed at the right edge of this present-day photo, looking to the left.

A graduation ceremony at the Occidental College Hall of Letters circa 1910.

The east side of the former Occidental College Hall of Letters as it appears today. The once proud college building and historic movie site now sits anonymously, barely half its former height.

I found this view at www.local.live.com, an Internet site that allows you to study low altitude aerial photos of nearly every spot where Chaplin filmed. The arrow marks the path Edna took from the "hospital." A former railroad right of way appears across the upper right corner. Occidental relocated to a larger campus site in Eagle Rock in 1914 because the noisy adjacent train tracks disrupted class and limited the potential for future expansion.

Madonna and Child—as Edna watches a wedding party, a circular leaded glass window illuminates behind her. Late in life, while he was married to his longtime wife Oona O'Neill (a woman 37 years his junior), Chaplin deleted this wedding scene from the film's reissue. Interestingly, the scene depicts an elderly gentleman marrying a much younger woman. This shot *(middle)* shows the couple departing from the street entrance of the Chaplin Studio screening room onto the La Brea sidewalk. The far right shot, taken during the production of *Modern Times* in 1936, shows how the door and window were later switched.

In the early 1930s, the south wing of the studio along La Brea was moved back several feet to accommodate the widening of the street. At that time, the window and door openings were reversed, so that the doorway now leads into the studio projection booth instead of the screening room. Given that movie stock at the time was highly flammable, perhaps the change was made for safety reasons.

This circa-1918 view of the studio screening room matches the frame. In both this photo and during a scene from a later film, *A Woman of Paris*, the window opening to the left of the screening room door is rectangular. This means that the curved top of the arched window appearing in this scene with Edna *(above)* was a prop temporarily added to the wall.

Edna abandons her child in a wealthy family's limousine. The mansion is located at 55 Fremont Place, at the southwest corner of West Eight Street, south of Wilshire. The limousine was said to have been borrowed from director D.W. Griffith. Griffith was one of Chaplin's partners, along with Chaplin's actor friends, Douglas Fairbanks and Mary Pickford, who formed United Artists in 1919.

Chaplin no doubt became aware of this site because it sits across the street from where Mary Pickford once lived. In August 1918, Mary leased the palatial home of Helen Mathewson, located at 56 Fremont Place. Mary lived here with her mother, her sister Lottie, Lottie's daughter, Mary Pickford Rupp, and Mary's brother Jack following his return from the Great War. By August 1919 Mary had moved from Fremont Place to the Clark residence on Westmoreland Place.

Looking west today at 55 Fremont Place. The 10,000-square-foot home has nine bedrooms and six baths, and was recently owned by legendary prizefighter Muhammad Ali.

Panic-stricken, Edna questions the chauffeur about her missing child. This view shows the curved porch on the south end of the home.

Fremont Place was an exclusive gated community established in 1911. The star *(inset)* marks 55 Fremont Place as it appears in the film. In the background are the Rancho La Brea oil fields. The white arrow *(below)* points up La Brea, the street on which the Chaplin Studio is located several blocks to the north. The left oval marks the world famous La Brea Tar Pits on Wilshire near Fairfax, where fossils of Ice Age animals, including saber-toothed cats and wooly mammoths, were found trapped in the sticky tar, while the right oval marks the future site of the popular Farmer's Market, which opened in 1934 at 3rd and Fairfax.

Two car thieves case the joint. The circle marks the distinctive entrance gate to the Fremont Place community that appears *(below)* in *The Idle Class*.

This shot of the thieves driving away looks east down West Eighth Street at the back of 55 Fremont Place, the same house featured earlier from the front. The directional arrow matches the arrow below. The rectangle marks the former home of Mary Pickford at 56 Fremont Place.

This view of Charlie by the Fremont Place gate on Wilshire appears in *The Idle Class*.

Paul Ayers discovered the mansion by spotting it *(bottom center)* in this 1970s aerial view of Fremont Place. The circle marks the gate.

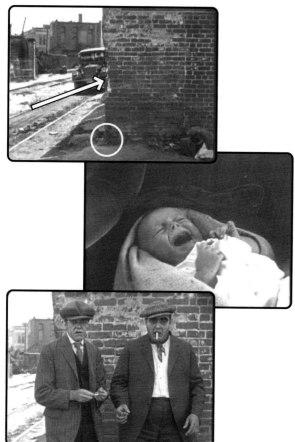

This 1920s aerial view looks east of the Plaza de Los Angeles. The circle marks the spot off of Alameda where the car thieves abandon the baby. The arrow marks the dual railroad tracks splitting off from the main rail line running up and down Alameda. Los Angeles Street runs across the photo, while the dotted line runs along the remains of what was then called Negro Alley (Calle de Los Negros), the original southern entrance to the plaza before Los Angeles Street was extended into the plaza in 1887. The Rescue Mission building (star) facing Negro Alley had a large courtyard in the back (ellipse). The left side of this courtyard was flanked by a twin row of

narrow buildings that were constructed specifically for prostitution (see more on later pages).

Negro Alley was the most notorious part of town, crammed with saloons, sporting houses, and opium dens, and was the site of a terrible tragedy known as the Chinese Massacre. Most residents of Chinatown were male immigrants, and for a long time very few women lived there. In October 1871, an altercation over a beautiful woman between two rival Chinese tongs lead to the accidental shooting of a white police officer. An outraged mob of 500 whites descended on Chinatown, murdering 19 Chinese men and boys, most of them by hanging.

The Chinese continued to endure many hardships, including the Chinese Exclusion Act of 1882 that prohibited Chinese laborers from entering the country, and related laws and restrictive covenants that prohibiting them from owning land. Today, the Chinese American Museum, standing within the remains of the Garnier Building (triangle) at 423 Los Angeles Street, honors their past sacrifices.

The upper right frame shows the thieves arriving by car. They are driving up an alley containing dual railroad tracks. The circle and arrow correspond to the aerial view. Below, the thieves appear startled by the sound of the crying infant.

This 1920 map, looking south, shows the dual train tracks splitting off of Alameda to run along a narrow alley. The star, appearing again on the next page, marks the courtyard behind the Rescue Mission building. The circle marks where the thieves stood at the end of the narrow twin rows of prostitution buildings.

This circa 1930 view shows the tracks splitting off from Alameda (*arrow*) and the court yard behind the Mission Rescue (*star*). The circle marks the approximate spot where the car thieves stood at the end of the narrow twin rows of prostitution buildings, although by the time this photo was taken a small two-story structure was built on the spot.

This view looks at the back of the Rescue Mission. The individual rooms running along the right edge, each with a single window and door, were constructed especially for prostitution. A second row of rooms stood further right, creating a narrow alley between them.

This photo shows the alley between the twin rows of prostitution rooms to the right of the Rescue Mission courtyard (*left*). The ellipse suggests where the car thieves stood a few yards away, at the end of these two rows of buildings.

Charlie Chaplin was so popular that other comedians made careers imitating Chaplin on film to help meet the demand. One of the best Chaplin imitators was Billy West. These two frames filmed within the Rescue Mission courtyard are from the Billy West 1918 short film *Playmates*, co-starring Oliver Hardy years before he teamed up with partner Stan Laurel.

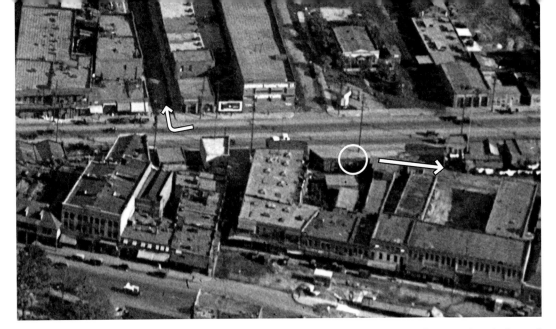

The thieves decide to abandon the baby, then speed off down Napier, a street off of Alameda in the heart of Chinatown. Notice the shadow of a RR crossing sign on the sidewalk, my first clue that this was filmed off of Alameda. Although dozens of trolley lines crisscrossed Los Angeles, only rail lines were designated with crossing signs. One of the primary rail lines into Los Angeles ran along Alameda.

The curved arrow shows the path of the car from Alameda onto Napier, close to the circle and arrow indicating where the thieves first discovered the baby.

These similar views look east down Napier from Alameda.

This production still *(left)* shows the setting where Charlie first discovers the abandoned baby, matching the frame *(upper right)*. By studying the frames closely, you can tell that a later shot *(lower left)* was filmed in reverse angle at the same spot. Although I have not been able to identify this location, it appears to me to be the identical setting used in Buster Keaton's 1920 short film, *Neighbors (lower right)*. The arrow in each frame points in the same direction. If you study the unique construction of the two-story building, with its exposed beam supported by round poles and overhanging some type of brick kiln, as well as its relation to the foreground wooden shed and the brick sheds across the dirt alley, the elements from the Chaplin shot and the Keaton shot seem to match exactly.

Desperate over her plight, Edna contemplates suicide. This scene was filmed at the Colorado Street Bridge in Pasadena. Built in 1913, the bridge spans the Arroyo Seco Canyon 160 feet below. It is believed to be one of the largest curved span bridges in the United States. With more than 100 known suicides, the bridge is known as "Suicide Bridge," and was remodeled with a suicide prevention fence. A vintage view appears lower right.

As Jackie scopes out the next window to break, policeman Tom Wilson gives him a questioning look. The background for these scenes is the Chin Woo building, built some time after 1907, located on the west side of Juan Street between Marchessault and Apablasa. The composite at the upper right shows Jackie running down Juan towards the corner of Marchessault. The arrow in each image points to the same doorway. The photo at the lower right shows the Juan/Apablasa corner of the building. The ellipse marks where Chaplin filmed a scene from *Police (lower left)*.

This view shows the Tin How Mui Temple located at the northwest corner of Juan and Apablasa Streets, where Jackie meets the cop across the street from the Chin Woo building. The circle marks the fire hydrant appearing in the scene *(upper right)*. The trio of triangular roof ornamentations would be removed by the 1930s *(see next page)*. Whether Chinatown deserved its reputation in the press as a hotbed of crime and vice is unclear. Yet newspaper accounts tell that on Juan Street, next door to where little Jackie Coogan filmed his scenes, (i) a shopowner was murdered by a rival tong in 1921, (ii) an opium den was raided by the police in 1923, and (iii) a gambling den was raided in 1928.

In this earlier view, a pair of gentlemen sun themselves on a bench while watching a group of traditionally dressed Chinese cross Apablasa Street.

Looking north from Napier Street, this view *(right)* shows the Marchessault side of the Chin Woo building to the left. The arrow marks the far corner of the Tin How Mui Temple where Jackie meets the cop. Chinatown was the home of a huge vegetable market where traveling merchants would collect their wares to sell door to door. The vacant lot in the foreground was used by the traveling Chinese merchants to park their vegetable wagons.

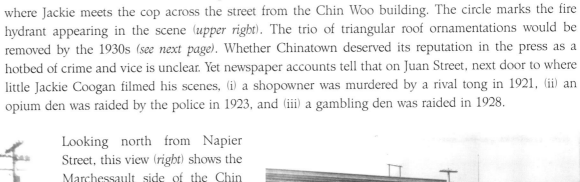

This view looks north up Juan, from Marchessault, towards Apablasa. Jackie and the cop stood around the corner marked by the arrow. By this point the triangular roof ornamentations have been removed from the top of the building.

This 1930s view was taken in preparation for the demolition of Chinatown to accommodate the new Union Train Station. The ellipse marks the corner of Juan and Apablasa where Jackie meets the cop. In all three circa-1930s photos on this page, the distinctive trio of triangular roof ornamentations (seen in earlier photos of the Tin How Mui Temple) have been removed.

This view looks east down Apablasa. The rectangle marks the corner where Jackie met the cop. In the foreground you can see a children's slide as part of some type of school or playground.

This frame from an early Charley Chase comedy for the Keystone Studio shows a similar view north up Juan Street looking towards Apablasa. Jackie and the cop stood around the corner marked by the arrow.

The Kid made Jackie Coogan a huge star. His little waif character was so popular that enterprising filmmakers quickly produced a series of movies in which Jackie played a similar role, that of the good-hearted street urchin who ultimately finds a loving (and often wealthy) family. Shortly after *The Kid* appeared, Sol Lesser released the feature *My Boy* (1921) as a starring vehicle for Jackie. Decades later, Jackie would regain some fame playing Uncle Fester in the macabre 1960s sitcom, *The Addams Family.*

My Boy was co-directed by Albert Austin, a Chaplin Studio character actor and assistant director. Although I cannot identify the location, the frame *(upper left)* from *The Kid*, and the frame *(upper right)* from *My Boy* were filmed at the same spot. The rectangle in the right frame marks the point of view in the left frame. Given that Albert Austin worked on *The Kid*, he likely chose to return to this spot when filming *My Boy*. Scenes from a later Jackie Coogan movie, *The Rag Man* (1925), also correspond to settings from *The Kid.*

Jackie Coogan's father Jack was an eccentric dancer and comedian. The lower left frame shows him in the Roscoe "Fatty" Arbuckle–Buster Keaton short film, *Back Stage* (1919). Jack played three small roles in *The Kid*, first as a guest at a black-tie party, next as a flophouse pickpocket, and last, during a dream sequence, as the devil. The young angel being urged by Jack to flirt with Charlie is 12-year-old Lita Grey, who would become Chaplin's second wife in 1924.

This rare frame shows Buster Keaton waiting on Chaplin and Jackie Coogan during a publicity dinner shot for the First National promotional film, *Seeing Stars* (circa 1922). Director Thomas Ince stands to the left of Buster while actress Anita Stewart stands to Buster's right. To Anita's right is director Marshall Neilan. The woman sitting second from the right is Buster's sister-in-law, actress Norma Talmadge, and to the far right may be Norma's sister, actress Constance Talmadge. Presumably the man in the center is some First National bigwig. The film is featured on Laughsmith Entertainment's *Industrial Strength Keaton* DVD.

Charlie's anguish is almost too unbearable to watch as he realizes Jackie has been taken from him. Below in the orphanage truck, Jackie pleads for Charlie to save him. Charlie breaks free from the police and escapes to the roof determined to rescue Jackie. The ensuing rooftop chase was filmed on Ducommun Street off of Alameda, a bit east and south of the plaza.

The 3-D map below comes from a large 1908 panoramic map of Los Angeles. The ellipse shows the houses featured in the chase, beginning with an unusually narrow triangle building at the west end, and a large, square two-story house at the east end. The alley behind the houses was called Labory Lane, where Charlie jumps into the moving orphanage truck. The corner of Alameda and Ducommun (star) was a popular filming location (right). The L.A. Farming and Milling Co. on the old map was later named the Globe A-1 Flour Mill.

The chase begins with Charlie moving east down Ducommun from the west end of the street near the triangle building, and then moving back and forth down the street depending on the shot.

Ducommun Street was named for Charles Louis Ducommun, a Swiss immigrant merchant who migrated to town in 1849. Catering to cattlemen and Gold Rush prospectors, he developed a hardware business and eventually became a supplier to industry. Ducommun Industries, originally founded in 1849, now supports the aerospace and wireless communications industries, and is the oldest company in California.

The Globe A-1 Flour Mill appears in the background of these scenes filmed at the corner of Alameda and Ducommun (star on map): Buster Keaton's The Goat (left) and Cops (bottom), along with Larry Semon's Frauds and Frenzies (middle). All were filmed a few steps from where Chaplin begins the rooftop chase.

A. This off camera still (A), looking north from the alley Labory Lane, shows the back of 420 Ducommun Street to the left (the "First House"), the first house east of the narrow triangle building starting the street, and the back of 424 Ducommun to the right (the "Second House"). Rollie Totheroh is standing next to Chaplin on the roof of the First House.

According to newspaper accounts, a decade earlier the Second House was raided by the police "purity squad." Before the police could capture her, the house madam climbed through a trap door where she hid in a garret concealed in the ceiling. I can imagine this episode appearing similar to Charlie's confrontation with the police as depicted in the movie.

B. The chase begins (B) with Charlie climbing eastward along the First House roof. Notice the empty steel frame behind him—this superstructure supported one of the gas holding tanks further down the street. The level of the tanks would rise and fall with use. The First House chimney (*rectangle*) is blocked from view behind Chaplin in still (A).

C. The chase continues eastward, in this shot looking west (C), as Charlie hangs onto the Second House chimney, the same chimney as circled in (A). The non-shingled roof to the left of Chaplin is a warehouse situated on Labory Lane visible in later shots. Despite appearances during the chase, the individual free-standing homes were not connected. Thus, there was no way for the policeman to traverse from his house to Charlie's without great risk.

D. Looking east, the chase continues as Charlie climbs the Second House roof where its staggered ridge lines meet (D). In the still (E), Charlie is standing on the Second House at this same spot of the narrow triangle building starting the street.

E. The Second House chimney (ellipse) in the foreground of still (E) is the same chimney (ellipse) appearing in (F, above), and in (A) and (C) on the prior page. The square-shaped two story house left of Chaplin's head was a duplex located at 450-452 Ducommun. It appears in scenes from Buster Keaton's *The Goat* (see next pages). In the far right background, the tall white building with the dark triangular roofs right of Chaplin is the Amelia Street Public School, another prominent landmark (see next page). The 300-foot-tall gas holder tank at the far left was the world's largest at the time it was built in 1912. By 1926, two even larger tanks would be built in front of it (see all three tanks on next page). The towers were part of a gas manufacturing complex Chaplin used for settings in *Modern Times*.

F. Chaplin now appears back at the First House where he started (F), as he spies the approaching orphanage truck traveling west down Labory Lane. The First House chimney in the foreground (rectangle) is the same chimney (rectangle) in (B). The chimney (ellipse) in the foreground of (E) appears by Chaplin's feet in (F).

Harold Lloyd, close by on Jackson Street, films a scene from *For Heaven's Sake* (1926), with the Amelia Street School in the background. The right gas storage tank *(rectangle)* on the north side of Jackson Street also appeared in *Modern Times*, as Charlie is driven off to a mental hospital *(lower left)*. The mostly Asian onlookers presumably lived nearby. The inset shot shows Harold standing next to director Sam Taylor.

This view down Labory Lane also shows the Amelia Street School *(lower right)*.

Here are more scenes filmed at the corner of Alameda and Ducommun mentioned earlier, only this time looking east down Ducommun. The inset view from Buster Keaton's short film *Cops (above)* provides a clear view of the narrow triangle building. The arrow marks the First House, behind the triangle building, where Chaplin begins the chase at 420 Ducommun *(B)*. The arrow below from Buster Keaton's *The Goat* marks the large square duplex house at 450–452 Ducommun appearing behind Chaplin *(E)*.

This composite frame from an early silent film documentary looks east down Ducommun to the left, and Labory Lane to the right. The arrow marks the warehouse appearing to the left of Chaplin in *(C)*. The Ducommun triangle building also appears in this Keystone film, *Call a Cop* (1921) *(middle)*. The view east down Ducommun from Alameda as it appears today *(lower right)*.

Charlie now appears further east down the street, running across the roof of a duplex, 434–436 Ducommun *(upper left and composite stills above)*, continuing along the same low roof to where it meets the back of the alley *(lower left)*, allowing him a perch for leaping into the oncoming orphanage truck. While Chaplin obviously performed this stunt, notice how unnaturally close the truck is driving along the fence, minimizing the distance Chaplin was forced to leap. The narrow chimney behind Charlie in the upper left frame and the odd ventilation box above Charlie in the lower left frame appear together in the movie frame taken from the First House *(ellipse, middle left)*.

After pushing the orphanage official from the truck, Charlie and Jackie pass behind the Baker Building (*right*) as they turn south onto Arcadia. Sanchez Street (*see* Police *chapter*) appears in the far background.

Built in 1878 by Col. Robert S. Baker for his wife Arcadia (*see* Police *chapter*), the Baker Building, located one block south of the plaza, was the

grandest building in Southern California. The entire façade was made of cast iron plates, and a large wooden awning surrounded the shops on the first floor. The central entryway facing Main Street featured an enormous grand double staircase flanking both sides of the lobby. Lawyers, physicians, and prominent business people rented offices on the second floor, while the top floor contained fashionable apartment suites. Its elaborate cupola towers were a prominent early landmark. In its final years it served as the headquarters for Good Will Industries before it was demolished to make way for the Santa Ana Freeway.

This same alleyway appears in two later Jackie Coogan films: during a chase scene in *My Boy* (1921) to the left and as Jackie sells scrap items in *The Rag Man* (1925) to the right. The alley was quite narrow, and could be closed shut by drawing down a vertical gate. Chaplin framed his shot (*above*) in a way to make it appear more like a true street corner. Notice that Chaplin's slim truck is barely two seats wide—a normal-sized truck would have had trouble negotiating the tight corner.

The arrow in each photo shows the direction of Chaplin's truck as it exits the alley from behind the Baker Building onto Arcadia. This aerial 1920s view looks east. The Baker Building appears in the lower right corner.

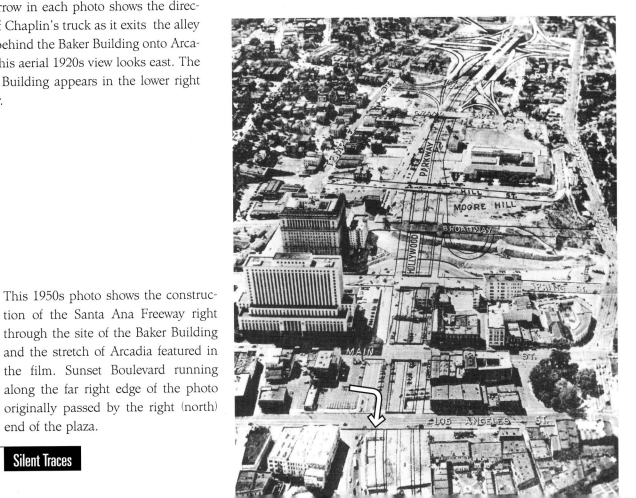

This 1950s photo shows the construction of the Santa Ana Freeway right through the site of the Baker Building and the stretch of Arcadia featured in the film. Sunset Boulevard running along the far right edge of the photo originally passed by the right (north) end of the plaza.

These movie frames show the alley entrance onto Arcadia as it appears in *The Kid (top)*, in Harry Langdon's 1927 feature film *Long Pants (middle)*, and as Buster Keaton runs down Arcadia Street from Main Street in *Cops (1922) (bottom)*.

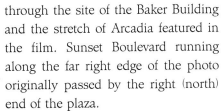

Crowning a desperate and heroic rescue, Charlie and Jackie's heart-tugging reunion is one of the most emotionally charged scenes in film history. Their poignant reunion takes place on Olvera Street, along the same spot where Chaplin earlier filmed a chase scene from *Easy Street*.

This early view shows Olvera Street being paved prior to its renovation. The circle marks the distinctive twin windows appearing in the frame and the view today *(right)*.

Today, Olvera Street remains a popular tourist attraction. Gerald Smith, Bonnie McCourt, and David Totheroh found this location, in part, from clues revealed during a 1964 family interview with David's grandfather.

Full of righteous bravado, Charlie chases off the frightened truck driver. This composite frame looks south down Olvera Street towards the trees in the plaza in the far background. The balcony to the left of Chaplin is the back of the Sepulveda House (1887), today home to the El Pueblo Visitors Center.

The balcony appearing above Chaplin's head is the Pelanconi House. Built around 1855–87, it is the oldest brick building in the city. Today it is home to the La Golondrina Cafe, founded by Consuelo Castilo de Bonzo, which has operated there since the opening of Olvera Street in 1930. At a time when most Mexican restaurants were self-described "Spanish kitchens," the Golondrina claims to be the first city restaurant to serve food identified as "Mexican" rather than "Spanish" in origin.

The vintage photo was taken shortly after Olvera Street opened in 1930, and matches the view above.

This pre-1930 photo shows the Pelanconi House in the foreground, and the recently completed City Hall in the background. This photo was taken before the street was graded and paved as part of the Olvera Street redevelopment.

This view west down Apablasa Street shows the corner of Cayetano Alley *(ellipse)* where Chaplin stood in the frame. The ellipse in each image marks the same corner. According to records provided by Jeffrey Vance, Edna's mansion was likely located near Wilshire and Wilshire Place, and is apparently now replaced by a commercial building.

In the film's closing scene, the police pick up Charlie and reunite him with Jackie at Edna's mansion. Charlie is standing at the corner of Cayetano Alley on Apablasa Street. The building with the balcony *(arrow)* is 328 Apablasa. This composite image incorporates a 1934 charcoal sketch by John W. Wardman made at the same spot, showing more of the block as well as the future position of City Hall, which opened in 1928. Wardman created an entire series of evocative sketches of Chinatown before it was torn down.

This 1930s aerial view looks north toward the corner of Cayetano Alley *(ellipse)*.

This detailed view shows the building *(arrow)* appearing in the above frame. It comes from this composite view *(inset)* looking west down Apablasa to the right from the corner of Juan. Shops identified as 330 and 328 Apablasa appear in the right background.

This 1930s aerial view, looking west, was taken after part of Chinatown had already been demolished to make way for the Union Train Station, and shows where all of these scenes were filmed. Alameda is the major street running across the bottom third of the photo. Los Angeles Street and Main Street run along the bottom and top, respectively, of the plaza in the center.

The Idle Class

Released September 25, 1921

Chaplin plays dual roles, the Little Tramp and a wealthy, neglectful husband to Edna Purviance. The film opens at the former Pasadena train station with the idle rich departing from their first-class cabins and the idle poor (Charlie) departing from an undercarriage baggage compartment. I discovered this location by noticing the station reflected in the window of the arriving train. Reversing the image *(inset, below)* you can clearly read "PASADENA."

These matching frames compare how the station appeared when Chaplin filmed in 1921, and in Buster Keaton's 1925 feature film, *Go West*. The two top shots look south down the rail line, the Chaplin frame to the left. Matching buildings *(arrows)* appear in each shot. A newer building constructed after 1921 appears to the right of the arrow in the Keaton frame.

The lower left Chaplin frame looks to the north end of the station, while the Keaton lower right frame looks south towards the same spot. The arrows identify the station sign and lamppost appearing from different angles in both shots.

The Pasadena Santa Fe Train Station first opened in 1887, welcoming wealthy Easterners who spent their winters at posh hotels under the warm California sun. Today, the modern Metro Gold Line urban transit runs along the same rail right-of-way.

Buster Keaton also filmed scenes here for his 1921 short film *The Goat* *(lower left)* at nearly the same time as when Chaplin filmed here. You can see from the above photo where Chaplin's scene *(lower middle)* and Keaton's scene were both shot.

Visible in the background of the station is the Castle Green *(arrow)*, a delightful Moorish- and Spanish-style hotel built in 1897. Castle Green is a popular movie location, appearing in such films as *Bugsy* (1991). Converted into apartments, the Castle Green is listed on the National Register of Historic Places, and is located at 99 South Raymond Avenue in Pasadena. The small foreground tower *(lower right)* was once part of a pedestrian bridge leading across the street to another hotel.

This next shot shows Charlie apparently leaving the Pasadena train station. Although the station was situated beside two large first-class hotels, Chaplin filmed this shot 15 miles away beside this decorative entrance gate to Fremont Place. Chaplin used this posh neighborhood just south of Wilshire Boulevard for the abandoned baby scene from his immediately prior film, *The Kid*. Paul Ayers discovered this setting.

This aerial view shows the Fremont Place gates (*ellipse*) in relation to the mansion Chaplin used in *The Kid*. The arrow shows the camera's point of view (*lower left*) filming the car thieves. The gate (*arrow below*) appears behind the thieves in this movie frame from *The Kid*.

Charlie takes up a leisurely round of golf near the first hole at what is now the Wilson Golf Course in Griffith Park. You can see a bit of Glendale in the background between the bush and Chaplin's head *(above)*. The rectangle marks a section of ridgelines in the movie frame corresponding to the modern view looking southeast towards Glendale *(upper right)*. The arrow matches a similar feature in the vintage photo *(lower left)*. Notice the dirt fairways in the vintage view, and that no golf carts are being used. Paul Ayers discovered these three golf course settings.

Located a few miles northwest of Downtown Los Angeles, Griffith Park is the largest municipal park in the country, created from 3,500 acres of land donated to the city by Griffith J. Griffith in 1896. A Welsh immigrant who made a vast fortune speculating in mining ventures, Griffith was well-known as an eccentric egomaniac. In 1903, Griffith became convinced that his Catholic wife and the Pope were conspiring to poison him, and he shot her in a drunken, delusional rage, blinding her in one eye.

Pleading alcoholic insanity in his defense, Griffith served over two years in San Quentin. A pariah after his release, the city spurned Griffith's further gifts until his death in 1919, when the city reluctantly accepted a bequest used to build the Griffith Observatory, completed in 1935. Aside from the observatory, the park features bridle paths, miniature train rides, the Travel Town transportation museum, the Autry Museum of Western Heritage, the Los Angeles Zoo, and four golf courses.

Taken near the same spot as on the prior page, this view looks more directly east towards Glendale.

The rectangle in this modern view shows the ridgelines of the Verdugo Hills, the Flintridge Hills, and the San Gabriel Mountains corresponding to the movie frame. The present-day trees and other vegetation, after more than 80 years' growth, prevent taking a shot directly corresponding to the movie frame.

Looking to the northwest, Charlie walks along the north bank of the Los Angeles River, a bit west from the Los Feliz Boulevard crossing. At the time Chaplin filmed here, the river had not been paved over.

Originally called Shale Hill, the background hill is named Beacon Hill for the aviation beacon that once stood there to guide aviators landing at the Grand Central Airfield in Glendale. A 1933–34 winter deluge led to the construction, beginning in 1938, of the cement-lined flood control channel that today replaces most of the natural river.

Charlie arrives on the grounds of the Beverly Hills Hotel. The ellipse in this 1920s photo *(right)* marks the portion of the driveway arcade appearing behind Chaplin in the movie frame.

The hotel driveway entrance today *(left)*. A large east wing, added in 1950, fills most of the area where the arcade stood. Edna arrives at the hotel *(above)* further down the driveway. The rectangle marks the same lamppost in the photo *(upper right)* and in the frame.

In 1906, developer Burton Green, head of the Rodeo Land and Water Company, acquired what had been a Mexican-era rancho, and named it Beverly after his home in Beverly Farms, Massachusetts. In 1907, he changed the name to Beverly Hills. The upper photo was taken shortly after the Beverly Hills Hotel opened in 1912. Green built the 300-room hotel on former bean and grain fields north of Sunset Boulevard at a reported cost of $500,000 (!), in part as a magnet for his then-isolated housing development.

The hotel was originally owned and managed by Mrs. Margaret Anderson and her son Stanley, and it immediately became a chic meeting place for the Hollywood elite. The Mission Revival-style hotel was renovated in the 1940s with a pink and green motif, earning it the nickname "The Pink Palace." This cultural icon is now owned by the Sultan of Brunei, reportedly the wealthiest man in the world.

Mrs. Anderson had previously leased the famous Hollywood Hotel (see Tillie chapter) from owner Mira Hershey, and had managed it for 10 years. In a remarkable dispute, Mrs. Anderson closed the Hollywood Hotel down when its lease expired, and bussed all 200 guests to the Beverly Hills Hotel that had just opened the day before. The Hollywood Hotel quickly re-opened under new management.

The Beverly Hills Hotel has appeared in dozens of films. The hotel front lawn appears in this introductory shot (left) from Harold Lloyd's 1921 four-reel film, A Sailor-Made Man.

Chased by the police, a wary Charlie (right) checks his bearings. The end of the hotel arcade (ellipse) appears in the frame and in the photo (above).

Charlie and a proper gentleman share a bench beside the Sunset Park fountain. Charlie and the gentleman *(below)* both seem surprised by the wandering fingers of a pickpocket hiding behind their bench.

Beverly Hills's first park, Sunset Park opened across Sunset Boulevard from the hotel in 1915. It was here that Will Rogers was named Beverly Hills's first honorary mayor in 1926. The park was renamed Will Rogers Memorial Park in 1952, 17 years after his death in a plane crash with aviator Wiley Post. The view of the central fountain *(above)* matches the movie frames *(right)*.

Chaplin used the park's twisting corners and pathways to good advantage. Here Charlie and a pursuing policeman encounter each other at a path's juncture. The dotted line marks the row of palm trees lining the park's central path *(dotted line)* on the vintage aerial photo of the park *(right)*. The arrow in the frame and in the vintage photo mark the same point of view. Today *(right)*, after 80 years' growth, the park resembles a verdant forest.

The parkside chase continues, with views looking west *(upper left)* and northeast *(lower left)*, and their corresponding views today.

Abject, Charlie leaves the hotel grounds. Visible through the taxi windows is the tile roof of a small trolley stop facing Sunset Boulevard *(arrow, rectangle, right)*.

The hotel served as a setting *(lower left)* for this 1917 Mack Sennett comedy, *Teddy at the Throttle*. The ellipse encircling Bobby Vernon on the tennis courts corresponds to the ellipse in the aerial photo *(upper right)*. To the lower right, Bobby Vernon and Gloria Swanson share a bench on the hotel grounds with the west side of the hotel in the background.

This 1918 aerial view of the hotel and park grounds shows where these eight scenes were filmed.

Charlie plays a construction hand, digging ditches and laying brick. On payday, Charlie spends his meager earnings in a bar, but must eventually return home to his virago of a wife.

The construction lot set *(ellipse)* appears in this aerial view of the Chaplin Studio *(bottom left)* taken during the production. This reaction shot of Mack Swain *(right)* reveals the studio tower *(rectangle)* and a circular air vent of the studio vault *(ellipse)* in the background. The rectangle within the view of Charlie leading a studio tour *(lower right)* corresponds to the view in the frame, looking west towards the studio gate.

Through reverse photography, Charlie appears to catch dozens of bricks that he in fact drops one by one *(middle left)*. Charlie toils in the trenches while the manager sits by idly *(middle right)*.

Charlie, an escaped convict disguised in a preacher's stolen clothes, is confronted at a small border-town train station by a congregation expecting the arrival of their new pastor. Charlie goes along with the ruse, delivering a stirring sermon in pantomime about David and Goliath. When a crook from Charlie's past steals a church member's mortgage money, Charlie recovers the funds but exposes his true identity. A kindly sheriff offers Charlie a chance to escape into Mexico. Torn between imprisonment on one side, and an ongoing bandito gunfight on the other, Charlie marches off into the sunset straddling the U.S.–Mexico border.

Always an outcast, Charlie plays an escaped convict in two films. This newspaper headline from *The Adventurer* describes Charlie's daring prison escape.

Criminal Escapes Convict At Large

Officials Completely Baffled

Rain of Bullets Fail to Stop Convict No. 23 in Wild Dash from State Prison. The most daring escape in the history of the State Prison was that today of Convict No. 23, known to the authorities as "The Eel," who gained his freedom after a mad dash through a shower of bullets and who had up in a late hour successfully covered every trace of his whereabouts.

This wanted poster from *The Pilgrim* describes Charlie as being only five feet, four inches, although many reliable sources, including Chaplin's son Charles, Jr., list him as being five foot, six-and-a-half inches. Chaplin's eyes were blue, though, as they were identified in the poster. I love the joke describing that the convict walks with his feet turned out.

$1,000 Reward Escaped Convict

May be disguised. 30 to 35 years of age. About five feet four inches tall in height. Weight about 125 pounds. *Pale face*. Black bushy hair sometimes parted in the middle. Small black mustache. Blue eyes. Small hands, *large feet*. Extremely nervous. *Walks with feet turned out*.

In disguise, Charlie walks along the Saugus train station. Gerald Smith first identified this setting by spotting the itinerary by the train station door.

A closer view of the station.

A 1931 view looking south down San Fernando Road in Saugus.

The Southern Pacific Saugus Train Station was originally located on the east side of San Fernando Road, just south of Drayton Street in what is now called Santa Clarita, a few miles east of the Six Flags Magic Mountain amusement park, about 40 miles from Downtown Los Angeles. Henry Newhall named the station after the Massachusetts town "Saugus" where his father was born.

The station was dedicated in 1887 by California Governor Washington Bartlett and Southern Pacific president David D. Colton. It was saved from demolition in 1980 when it was relocated three miles south to the Heritage Junction Historic Park, operated by the Santa Clarita Valley Historical Society, at 24107 San Fernando Road in Newhall. The park sits adjacent to the William S. Hart Regional Park, containing the former ranch and mansion of the famed silent film cowboy and movie director. The Saugus station has also appeared in such films as *Suddenly* (1954) starring Frank Sinatra, and more recently in *The Grifters* (1989) starring Angelica Huston, Annette Bening, and John Cusack.

Chaplin filmed *The Pilgrim* at three different train stations. My search started when Chaplin author Jeffrey Vance provided me a brief list of settings for this film culled from studio records. After investigating the cryptic word "Raymond," I found these confirming photos of the Raymond Depot online at the L.A. Public Library. After his arrival, Charlie and actor Mack Swain (*above*) stroll along the depot, situated southeast of where S. Raymond Avenue terminates at East Glenarm Street in Pasadena.

The former Raymond Station (*below*) was built in 1887 near the site of the old Raymond Hotel, just east of Fair Oaks. This sketch by Charles Owens appeared in the *Los Angeles Times* on June 17, 1938.

Looking south, this photo shows the east side of the Raymond Depot. Part of the old Raymond Hotel appears on the hill in the background. The ellipse matches the movie frame *(left)*.

Through the magic of film editing, Charlie and Mack continue their stroll, passing seamlessly from the Raymond Depot to the Raymond Station 50 yards further west. Notice the distinctive circular arch over their heads.

Looking west towards the Raymond Station, 1944.

This aerial view looking south toward the Raymond Hotel shows the relation of the Raymond Depot *(ellipse)* to the Raymond Station *(arrow)*. Located only yards apart, Chaplin and company simply picked up from the depot, and continued the shoot at the station.

This vintage aerial map shows the relation of the Pasadena Train Station on Raymond Avenue appearing in *The Idle Class (rectangle)* to the Raymond Station located only a few blocks further south *(arrow)*.

A Woman of Paris

In 1919, actors Charlie Chaplin, Douglas Fairbanks, Mary Pickford, and director D.W. Griffith formed their own movie production and distribution company called United Artists. Because Chaplin would take four more years to fulfill his remaining obligation to First National, he could not begin to supply films to United Artists until 1923. To the frustration of his partners, the first film Chaplin did produce was a self-entitled "drama of fate" in which Chaplin did not even appear. (However, Chaplin is believed to play an uncredited cameo as a baggage handler.)

Following *A Woman of Paris*, United Artists would produce all of Chaplin's remaining American films up through *Limelight* in 1952. Chaplin's final two films made in exile from the United States, *A King in New York* (1957) and *A Countess from Hong Kong* (1967), were produced through the Attica Film Company and Universal, respectively.

Chaplin created *A Woman of Paris* as a showcase for his maturing co-star and former lover Edna Purviance, hoping to establish her as an independent dramatic star. Edna plays Marie, a girl from a French village who plans to elope to Paris with her fiancé, Jean. Jean's father dies suddenly, however, preventing Jean from meeting Marie at the train station. Feeling snubbed, Marie leaves for Paris alone, where she becomes a mistress to wealthy bon vivant Pierre (Adolphe Menjou). By chance, Jean and Marie reunite a year later, tearing Marie between love and financial security. Despondent, Jean commits suicide. In atonement, Marie dedicates her life to caring for orphans. The film ends with Marie and Pierre passing each other unnoticed on a country lane, while Pierre's passenger inquires "Whatever became of Marie St. Clair?"

Gerald Smith first noticed that Marie and Jean stroll to the "train station" by walking past the Chaplin Studio gate (*above, behind Edna*) and screening room entrance (*far right edge*).

The same view of the studio today, at 1416 N. La Brea Avenue, in Hollywood.

Grim faced Jean (played by Carl Miller) takes a midnight stroll along the Colorado Street Bridge in Pasadena. Edna played a similar scene of despair at the Colorado Street Bridge in Chaplin's earlier film, *The Kid*.

To show her contempt, Marie tosses one of Pierre's expensive necklaces out into the street. When a bum stoops to pick it up, she madly dashes outside and snatches it back from him *(right)*.

The Robinson biography mentions that the swank apartment where Pierre keeps Marie was located near Westlake (now MacArthur) Park. Steve Vaught, a film historian and producer who is writing a book about classic Los Angeles hotels, homes, and apartments tentatively entitled *Historic Hollywood*, was up to the challenge. He spotted her apartment as the seven-story Ansonia Apartments located at 2205 West Sixth Street. The frame of Edna looks south down Lake Avenue towards the corner of Sixth. The north side of MacArthur Park appears at the end of the street. Steve writes that at the time of filming, Edna's real apartment was only a few blocks away at 402-B Alvarado Street, the infamous Alvarado Court Apartments where one of Hollywood's greatest unsolved mysteries took place, the murder of director William Desmond Taylor in 1922.

Today, little has changed. The author *(right)* beside the Ansonia Apartments.

The opening scenes *(lower left)* featured this rustic French village. This panoramic view of the Chaplin Studio, looking west, shows part of the garage at the left, and the rustic village set towards the right.

The Gold Rush

Released June 26, 1925

Charlie plays a lone prospector who strikes it rich in the Klondike gold rush. Recognized for scenes such as a famished Charlie feasting on a boiled boot, Charlie's cabin tilting over the edge of a cliff, and Charlie's "dance" of the dinner rolls, Chaplin described *The Gold Rush* as the film by which he'd most like to be remembered. The image of Chaplin *(below)* huddled from the cold, is one of his most famous. As a teenager I decorated my bedroom wall with a home-made poster of this image.

Chaplin performs his celebrated dance of the dinner rolls in the film *(above, right)* and during a party for a home movie *(above, center)*. The origin of the gag is not certain. Roscoe "Fatty" Arbuckle briefly performed the gag years earlier in his 1918 short *The Rough House*, but while imitating Chaplin's shuffle. Since Roscoe and Charlie worked together several times in 1914, it's possible either one could have learned the gag from the other. In any case, Chaplin's delightful and inimitable performance makes the gag forever his own.

Although Chaplin filmed exterior snow scenes near Truckee, California for nearly three weeks in April 1924, most of these shots were discarded and later re-created at the studio lot. One exterior shot to remain in the film was Chaplin's re-creation of the miners struggling over Chilkoot Pass *(upper right)*, inspired by real events in the Alaskan gold rush.

Chaplin biographer David Robinson quotes Chaplin's publicist Jim Tully, who wrote of the filming: "To make the pass, a pathway of 2,300 feet long was cut through the snows, rising to an ascent of 1,000 feet at an elevation of 9,850 feet. Winding through a narrow defile to the top of Mount Lincoln, the pass was only made possible because of the drifts of eternal snow . . . against a narrow basin, a natural formation known as the 'Sugar Bowl'."

Armed with these clues, Gerald Smith traveled to the Sugar Bowl Ski Resort, taking the Soda Springs/Norden exit off of I-80, and drove about three miles east, until the unmistakable ridgeline on Mt. Lincoln came into view. The Chilkoot Pass sequence was filmed against a distinctive rocky ridge called The Palisades, situated between Mt. Lincoln to the south and Mt. Disney to the west. To film the sequence, three carloads of hobos were brought in by train from Sacramento to work as extras. The setting is in the heart of what is today a modern ski resort built by Walt Disney in 1939.

The inset *(lower left)* shows Lita Grey in her role as the dance hall girl. She would soon become Chaplin's second wife, and would eventually be replaced by Georgia Hale in the cast.

The sequence where Charlie resorts to eating a boiled boot was inspired by real-life events. In May 1846, a wagon train of settlers known as the Donner Party left Missouri bound for California, only to be trapped months later in the Sierra Nevada by an early snow. Forced to endure the long winter with meager supplies, the pioneers slaughtered their oxen and ate anything else edible before eventually resorting to cannibalism. Only 46 of the original 87 pioneers survived. The Donner Party memorial site is situated just a few miles from where Chaplin filmed.

In April 2005, 90-year-old Jack Totheroh embarked on a weekend expedition retracing his father Rollie Totheroh's 1924 journey to Donner Summit to film Chaplin in *The Gold Rush*. Led by his son (Rollie's grandson) David, Jack and a small group rode an enclosed cab Sno-Cat tracker to the very spot where the Chilkoot Pass scene was filmed against the Sugar Bowl Palisades 81 years earlier.

Chaplin fans Gerald Smith, Christopher Snowden *(back)*, Bonnie McCourt, Jack Totheroh, Sugar Bowl Marketing Manager Kris York, David Totheroh, and Jack's wife Marian, stand before the Palisades, where Rollie Totheroh filmed Chaplin for the opening scene.

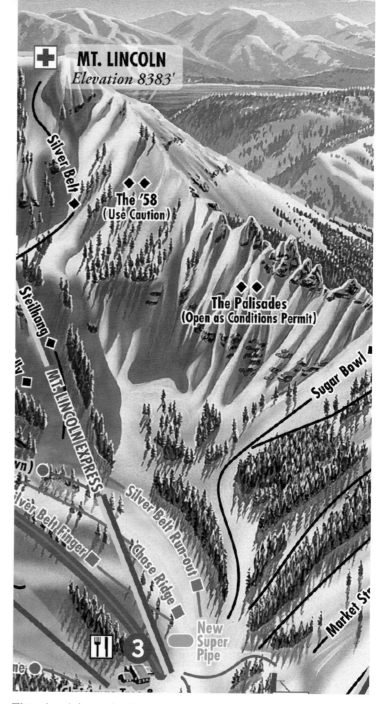

This detail from the Sugar Bowl trail map shows the relation of the Palisades to Mt. Lincoln. Chaplin's crew set up the tent village for the scene at the base of the Palisades.

This detail of the Sugar Bowl Ski Resort trail map shows the approximate spot where Chaplin stood, and where David Totheroh took the above photo.

The "Lone Prospector," Charlie scans the horizon. He is standing along the ridge between Mt. Lincoln and Mt. Judah. The ellipse in the present-day photo (right) marks his approximate location.

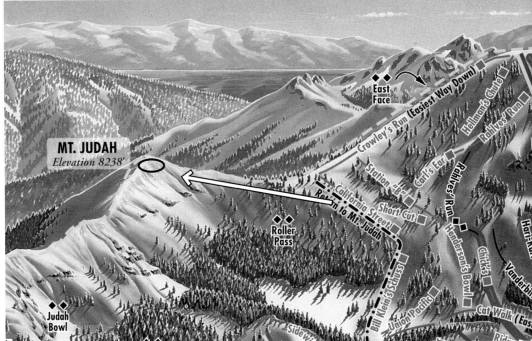

Near the same spot as above, Chaplin confers with principal cameraman (and unofficial assistant director) Rollie Totheroh. Their remarkable professional association is one of the longest in film history, beginning in 1916 with the Mutual film *The Floorwalker* and continuing until *Limelight* in 1952.

Another vintage view of the Summit Hotel where Chaplin and company stayed in April 1924 during the filming.

Following her appearance as the flirty angel in *The Kid*, in March 1924, Chaplin cast 15-year-old Lita Grey as the female lead in *The Gold Rush*, his first leading lady hired following Edna Purviance's lengthy tenure. During the filming, Chaplin and company stayed at the Summit Hotel, pictured here. In an oral history recorded by the Totheroh family, Rollie Totheroh recalls Charlie had a room at the hotel in between those used by Lita and her mother. By September that year, Lita was 16 and pregnant, and she and Chaplin quickly married in Mexico in November 1924. Due to Lita's pregnancy, Chaplin cast actress Georgia Hale to play the leading role instead. Lita and Charlie's 1927 divorce was one of the most bitter and scandalous in Hollywood history, the stress of which reportedly turned Chaplin's hair white.

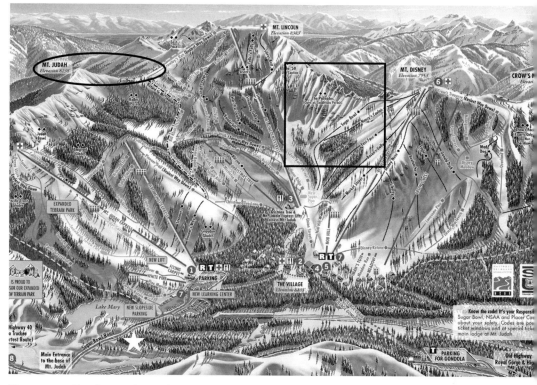

Downtown Truckee today *(left)* still honors its connection to Charlie Chaplin.

This overview of the Sugar Bowl Ski Resort shows the relation of the Palisades filming location *(rectangle)* to the Lone Prospector shots *(ellipse)* and the site of the former Summit Hotel in what is now the resort parking lot *(star)*.

The Circus

UNITED ARTISTS

Released January 6, 1928

Charlie falls in with a traveling circus, where his inadvertent antics make him the unwitting star of the show. Once there, Charlie is smitten with the lovely equestrienne played by Merna Kennedy. When Rex, the handsome King of the High Wire, joins the troupe, Charlie sees that Merna and Rex love each other, and selflessly helps them elope. Merna and Rex reconcile with Merna's stepfather, the circus owner, and plead with Charlie to join them as the circus readies to leave for the next town. Charlie stays behind instead, standing alone in a barren field as the circus wagons and his love roll away in the early dawn. The film fades out as Charlie strolls away towards the horizon.

In the opening scenes, Charlie and a pickpocket attempt to elude the police on an amusement park pier. Here, Charlie approaches the Noah's Ark fun house attraction.

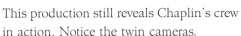

This production still reveals Chaplin's crew in action. Notice the twin cameras.

The Noah's Ark attraction was situated on the Venice Pier, and was rebuilt in 1921 following a disastrous fire.

The pickpocket (Steve Murphy) and the Little Tramp hide from the police by posing among the automatons in front of Noah's Ark. With the precise movements of a Swiss cuckoo clock, Charlie repeatedly conks his rival on the head, while the pickpocket, fearing arrest, has little choice but to play along.

This view shows the Noah's Ark attraction relative to the other attractions on the pier.

After dispatching the pickpocket, Charlie dashes to freedom.

The same setting appears in the 1927 Laurel and Hardy short film, *Sugar Daddies*.

Fleeing the police, Charlie turns a corner past a distinctive kiosk before heading east onto the pier midway. The Flying Circus attraction appears in the left background, while the Venice Dance Hall appears in the right background. The rectangle matches the building details in the adjoining frame *(right)*.

Looking south, this 1925 aerial view shows the length of the Venice pier, rebuilt in 1921 following a disastrous 1920 fire. The ellipse marks the location of Noah's Ark. The square marks the center of the midway, viewed in reverse angle in the frames above. The former Abbott Kinney Pier that once stood here appeared in Chaplin's early shorts, *By the Sea* and *The Adventurer*.

Character actor Steve Murphy is caught red-handed stealing from Charlie.

With his distinctive broken nose, Steve Murphy was born to play con men, thugs, and thieves. In this scene from Buster Keaton's short film *Cops* (1922), Steve is about to fleece Buster by selling him someone else's house full of furniture.

Charlie and Murphy both flee the police by racing east down the Venice Pier midway towards the mainland. The distinctive kiosk mentioned on the prior page appears in the background. The arrow points to the tail end of the Dragon Slide, a popular attraction where patrons would climb to the top of a tall tower and slide in the dark down a very long spiral track. The Chocolate Garden ice cream parlor (box) appears to the right.

This broad view of the midway reveals the full height of the Dragon Slide. The Chocolate Garden appears in the near foreground.

This production still shows that the scene on the prior page, and the hot dog scene below, were filmed on the Chaplin Studio open-air stage beside the east breezeway opening.

Charlie flees the police once again. I had actually searched through old amusement park photos hoping to spot this setting before discovering it was filmed on the studio lot.

This aerial photo of the Chaplin Studio shows the large, half circus tent set to the left, and the open-air stage where the hot dog scene was filmed to the right (arrow).

In this hysterical scene, Charlie adoringly makes play faces for a toddler while the other adults look on, and voraciously devours the infant's hot dog whenever the adults look away.

In this masterfully photographed sequence, Charlie encounters himself in a house of mirrors.

In a similar vein, Buster Keaton confronts his multiple image in this scene from his 1921 short film, *The Playhouse*.

Multiple exposure reveals Charlie's inner thoughts. Here he imagines giving the handsome wire walker Rex a good kick in the pants.

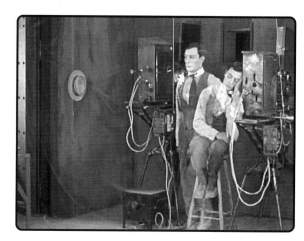

Keaton employed the same effect in *Sherlock Jr.* (1924), playing a sleeping theater projectionist who dreams himself into the movie he is showing.

This production still shows twin cameras filming Chaplin. This common practice assured that there would be two negatives, one that would be used to make prints for foreign distribution and the other for domestic prints.

CHAPLIN IN 3-D!

The Circus DVD supplement contains a side-by-side presentation of the images shot by Chaplin's twin A and B cameras. Anytime two images are taken side by side, they can be aligned to create a 3-D effect. To see Charlie in 3-D, look at one set of the twin spheres below the images, and relax your eyes, focusing beyond the page until you see four floating spheres. Manipulate the page, and your eyes, until the center two of the four spheres overlap. Once properly aligned, the small white circle will appear to float above the black circle. Then look up at the movie frames. You should see three photo images, the overlapping center image in 3-D.

Another method is to place the image behind a sheet of glass, and focus on your reflection instead of the image. Move the image either closer or away from your face, while focusing on your reflection, until the images overlap creating the 3-D effect. With either method, the trick is to focus beyond the page so that the right-hand image seen by your right eye, and the left-hand image seen by your left eye, overlap into a central 3-D image.

The 3-D images on the prior page, as well as the scenes on this page, appear in a deleted sequence where Charlie, Merna, and Rex meet at a cafe. The hilltop house in the background *(upper left)* located at 1331 Miller Drive is still standing *(see ellipse, photo, right)*.

En route to the cafe, Merna and Charlie stroll west along Sunset Boulevard. The Cafe La Boheme appearing in the background *(lower left)* was a popular Hollywood nightclub located at 8614 Sunset Boulevard, on the corner across the street from where Sunset Plaza Drive meets Sunset Boulevard *(lower right, today)*. The site would later become the Trocadero Ballroom, featured in the original 1937 version of *A Star is Born*. The trio strolls down Sunset past a short block of four commercial buildings that, though heavily remodeled, appear to be the same as in the film.

Charlie stands alone as his love and the circus leave him behind.

The climax of the movie was filmed in Glendale, near what is now Wilson Middle School. The studio records mention Chaplin filming the scene in Glendale. Paul Ayers speculated that because no major hills or mountains appear in the shots, the scenes must have been filmed looking south from the mouth of the Verdugo Canyon in Glendale towards the Los Angeles River. Noticing a road *(see passing car, circle, above right)* appearing in the background, Paul surmised that it might be Verdugo Road, which passes through Verdugo Canyon from Glendale to La Crescenta.

Verdugo Road was originally laid out in the early 19th century to run between the Pueblo de Los Angeles and the Verdugo family holdings in the Glendale area. By 1927, Verdugo Road had become the major thoroughfare for the developing communities of the La Crescenta Valley. Contemporary newspaper accounts confirmed Paul's theory, describing the filming as taking place at the "Thom property at the corner of Glendale and Verdugo," the site of "the Seventh-day Adventist encampment on Glendale Avenue." With these clues, Paul scouted the area for matching ridgelines. This still *(above right)* and the today shot *(right)* were taken looking south by south-east a bit below the present-day intersection of Glenoaks Boulevard and Adams Street in Glendale.

A studio crew member *(below)* watches the circus wagons heading down Verdugo Road in Glendale.

The general filming site, the playing field of Woodrow Wilson Middle School, bounded by Glenoaks Boulevard to the north (top), Verdugo Road (right), Adams Street (left), and Monterey Road (bottom).

Notice the very slight "saddle" in the ridgeline above Chaplin's head. The modern-day photo *(below)*, taken from the grounds of Wilson Middle School, shows Verdugo Road and the end of the ridgeline as it appears in the movie. Notice that Verdugo Road runs above the grade of the playing field. Verdugo Road can be seen running above-grade in the above still, and in the stills on the previous page.

Charlie walks off alone into the distance.

Chaplin was undoubtedly relieved to put this final shot in the can, as the entire production had been plagued by disaster and personal tribulations. During production, Chaplin endured the humiliation of a scandalous public divorce from Lita Grey in which his financial assets were frozen pending settlement. At the same time, Chaplin was investigated by the Internal Revenue Service, which placed liens against the studio.

As for the production, the film from the first month of shooting was ruined in the laboratory, and had to be shot over, while nine months into filming a fire swept the studio lot destroying props, costumes, and an interior stage.

The cumulative stress is said to have turned Chaplin's graying hair white. Even shooting the finale was problematic, as a group of college kids had stolen the circus wagons from the Glendale field the night before to use in a bonfire celebrating the UCLA–Occidental college football game. Fortunately, the wagons were recovered in time.

Despite the hardships, the results certainly merit the effort. On May 16, 1929, the first ever Special Achievement Award bestowed by the Academy of Motion Picture Arts and Sciences was presented to Chaplin "for versatility and genius in writing, acting, directing and producing *The Circus.*"

The hill with the water tank shown in the background (*arrow*) is Adams Hill adjacent to the Glendale Forest Lawn.

Charlie befriends a blind and impoverished flower girl (Virginia Cherrill), indulging her mistaken belief that he is a wealthy man. Charlie later saves a millionaire (Harry Myers) from killing himself, forging a schizophrenic relationship: while drunk the millionaire is Charlie's best pal, when sober, he doesn't recognize Charlie and scorns him. When Charlie learns an expensive operation will restore the flower girl's sight, he obtains the funds from the drunken millionaire. Once sober, the millionaire prosecutes Charlie, who is then imprisoned for theft.

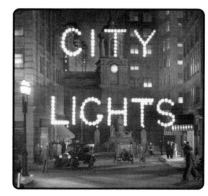

Released from prison years later, Charlie encounters the girl in front of her prosperous flower shop, her vision now fully restored. Taking pity on Charlie, she hands him a coin and a flower. At the touch of his hand, she suddenly realizes this broken man was her imagined wealthy benefactor, who has sacrificed everything for her. The movie concludes with nine marvelously nuanced words—"You can see now?" he asks. "Yes, I can see now." This heartrending, ambiguous ending remains one of the highlights of Chaplin's career, and of all cinema.

The film opens with this establishing shot of a busy city.

This rare production still shows that the city set was created using a hanging miniature—a scale model of the building tops hanging in the foreground designed to align with the full-scale street level sets in the background. Because the model and the set are filmed at the same time, the tones and lighting conditions match perfectly. The camera taking this still photograph was not properly aligned, as the elements within the rectangle are out of register.

In a priceless bit, the film opens as horrified civic leaders unveil a public monument, only to find Charlie coiled on the lap of Justice like a sleeping cat. As Charlie attempts to extricate himself (shown here in composite), he inadvertently defiles the statuary and mocks the crowd. Although filmed without dialog, a saxophone's muffled *womp-womp* sound perfectly suggests the pompous mayor's self-important speech. Chaplin took a huge risk filming the movie as a silent years after talkies had made such movies obsolete.

This related still shows the foreground model out of register with the real elements down the street. Even knowing how the effect is created it remains very difficult to discern.

This production still shows Chaplin blocking out the scene.

Chaplin agonized for months over how to convey in pantomime that the blind flower girl mistakes Charlie for a millionaire. His solution was for Charlie to make his way across bumper-to-bumper traffic by entering and exiting all the cars blocking his path. When the girl hears Char-

lie emerge from a limousine, she assumes that he must be wealthy. Charlie later reinforces her mistaken belief when he is able to pass along gifts received from his drunken millionaire friend.

Chaplin filmed his first encounter with the flower girl on the studio's open-air stage. Concentric circles of opposing traffic *(arrows)* continuously looped across the stage and back out onto the street to create a steady flow of cars in the background.

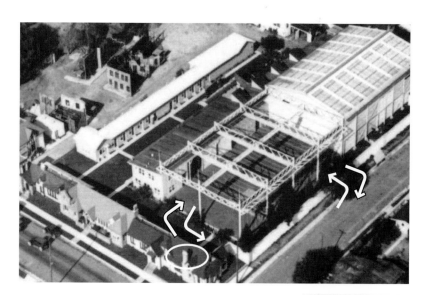

The open-air stage was located in the southwest corner of the studio. The twin chimney pipes to Chaplin's corner office *(upper ellipse)* appear in this photo to the right. The vertical ellipse marks the door to Chaplin's office. The frame *(lower left)* shows Chaplin busy directing the cast and crew. The first encounter between the Tramp and the flower girl was said to have taken months to film.

The *City Lights* park set is reminiscent of St. Mark's, on Kennington Park Road in London, between Braganza and Penton, where Chaplin had spent time as a boy *(lower right)*.

Though quite compact, the city set built at the studio afforded a number of different corners and vantage points from which to film. The arrow in this composite frame *(left)* matches the arrow on the aerial photo of the set *(below)*.

In an interesting reversal of perspective, the interior point of view shot of Charlie gazing at a nude statue *(above)* was filmed at the opposite end of the set from where the exterior view of Charlie apprising the statue *(right)* was filmed. The ellipses mark where Chaplin stood on the set, and the "Men's Furnishing" sign appearing behind him.

Having received a fistful of money from the drunken millionaire, Charlie rushes to the flower girl so that he may purchase her entire basket of flowers.

This scene was filmed in front of the Town House apartment building *(lower left)*, on the northwest corner of Wilshire Boulevard and Commonwealth Avenue.

This 1940s view *(lower right)* looks east down Wilshire Boulevard. Beyond the Town House lies Lafayette Park, where Chaplin likely filmed scenes for early movies, and to the far right, the Bryson Apartments appearing in *The Rink*.

During one memorable sequence, Charlie and the drunken millionaire drive home following a wild evening, each assuming the other is operating the car. Byrant Arnett first found these locations. Here, they drive past the corner of the J. W. Robinson Department Store, from Grand onto West Seventh heading northwest. Built in 1915, the store was remodeled in the Moderne style in 1934, changing the window pattern on the corner *(below)*.

The next shot was filmed a short block over, as they drive past the B.F. Coulter Dry Goods Company (built in 1917), and turn from West Seventh onto Olive heading southeast. The Ville de Paris Department Store in the background was used to film the department store interior shots appearing in Harold Lloyd's 1923 classic, *Safety Last*.

Heading west down Wilshire, with the prominent Gaylord Apartment building in the background, Charlie and the millionaire turn south onto Berendo, past the Immanuel Presbyterian Church. The street corner to the far left lies in front of the Talmadge Apartment house used by Buster Keaton as the setting for his father's mansion in *Battling Butler* (1926) (*lower right*). Buster's sister-in-law, silent film star Norma Talmadge, owned the building.

Charlie learns no one is in control of the car, and struggles for the wheel, as they turn from going west down Wilshire onto Rodeo Drive heading north. The Regent Beverly-Wilshire Hotel stands in the background.

Chaplin biographer David Robinson reported that after Chaplin replaced Henry Clive, the first actor hired to play the million-aire, Chaplin and replace-ment actor Harry Myers filmed a scene on the Pasadena Bridge in the early hours of July 11, 1929. Although this scene does not appear in the finished movie, this production still shows the actors at work on the bridge, the same setting Chaplin used twice before in *The Kid* and *A Woman of Paris* (right).

The same east breezeway studio door served as the "midway" set for *The Circus*. It appears (*ellipse*) in this view below.

With a defiant flick kick to his last cigarette, Charlie enters "prison" for turning the millionaire's money over to the flower girl.

This production still shows how the east studio breezeway was configured into a prison set. In the foreground lies part of the open-air stage where the cars circled each other during the scene when Charlie first meets the flower girl.

"You can see now?"
"Yes, I can see now."

Reportedly no production stills were taken during the concluding scene so that Chaplin could maintain secrecy regarding the production. This photo shows the now prosperous flower girl's shop window.

The arrow in this aerial shot matches the arrow *(above)*, showing where this famous scene was filmed. Chaplin would keep the set fairly intact for use in filming *Modern Times* and *The Great Dictator*.

Modern Times

Modern Times was released exactly five years after Chaplin's 1931 triumph, *City Lights*. While poverty and social issues frequently played roles in Chaplin's films, *Modern Times* was his first film to address the Great Depression and the dehumanizing effects of technology. Ironically titled, *Modern Times* was filmed without dialog, and is arguably the last commercially produced movie of the silent film era.

Tightening bolts on a relentless assembly line, Charlie the factory worker suffers a nervous breakdown. After recuperating in a sanatorium, he is mistaken for a labor agitator and sent to jail. Released for good behavior, Charlie seeks work on the waterfront. Missing the comforts of jail, Charlie volunteers to take the rap when a "Gamine" (played by Chaplin's third wife, Paulette Goddard) is caught stealing bread. Charlie and Paulette escape from the police, and work briefly at a department store, before residing together in a waterside shack. With the police on their trail, Charlie and Paulette flee to the open road. As the film fades out, Charlie encourages her to never give up, and hand-in-hand they walk bravely towards the future.

The film opens with the contrasting scenes of factory workers exiting a subway station and a herd of mindless sheep. A black sheep (the Tramp?) appears in the middle of the flock. Chaplin reminisced that as a boy he witnessed a lamb escape while it was being lead to a slaughterhouse near his home. Chaplin laughed as workers struggled with the errant lamb, only to cry once the captured lamb was sent to its slaughter. Chaplin speculated that this episode greatly influenced his views of tragedy and comedy.

Chaplin filmed this scene at a pedestrian tunnel crossing under Melrose Avenue at Formosa, seven blocks due south of the Chaplin Studio. The extras were sent the short distance in a fleet of buses. Chaplin directs the scene *(left)*.

Today, the underpass is fenced closed, presumably because it's now safer to risk the street traffic than to traverse a dark urban tunnel.

This special effects shot of the busy workers *(upper left)* used a matte painting to represent tall buildings in the background. This production still *(center)* shows how the scene looked without the effect. The scene was filmed on the Macy Street (now Cesar Chavez Avenue) Bridge, looking to the southwest. The view today *(right)* shows the Los Angeles City Records Center, at 555 Ramirez Street.

Factory worker Charlie tightens bolts on an ever-accelerating assembly line, eventually suffering a nervous breakdown. After attempting to tighten the buttons on a matron's dress, he is carted off to a sanatorium.

Contrasting images of man and machine; the right frame is from Buster Keaton's 1922 short, *Daydreams*.

Attracted by a matron's buttons, Charlie chases her west around the corner of Jackson Street, and north up Center Street.

This view north up Center Street shows the corner *(square)* of the Southern California Gas Company plant on Jackson Street appearing in the film. These three gigantic natural gas storage tanks dominated the city skyline for decades.

Bobby "Wheezer" Hutchins looks for his lost puppies at the northwest corner of Temple and Center in this frame from the 1930 Our Gang comedy, *Pups is Pups*. The rectangle behind him marks the corner Chaplin used *(above)*.

Character actress Juana Sutton marches purposefully east down Jackson Street from the central plant doorway. The directional arrow shows the point of view in the images *(upper right and lower left)*.

Before the advent of natural gas pipeline technology, gas was manufactured in Los Angeles by spraying water on burning coal. The first gas manufacturing plant was built in 1867, across the street from the Pico House on the plaza, supplying gas lights to the hotel guests. The Aliso Street gas manufacturing plant, where Chaplin filmed later scenes for this movie, first opened in 1876.

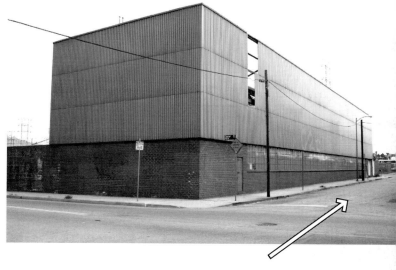

In 1927, Los Angeles switched from manufactured gas to natural gas imported from Texas and central California. As part of the larger Aliso Street facility, the Ducommun Street plant featured here housed steam-driven compressors that pumped the gas into the three large holding tanks. The Ducommun plant was upgraded in 1957 with modern turbo-gas compressors. Although similar in appearance to the original building, the compressor plant building pictured here was completely remodeled. This modern view shows the remains of the Ducommun Plant towards Center, past the plant's left doorway.

Charlie chases the matron west down Jackson Street. The railroad crossing sign *(circle)* warns of the train tracks running along the west bank of the Los Angeles River. The tower behind Chaplin's head held power lines aloft across the river.

Again from *Pups is Pups*, Wheezer's puppies dash across the train tracks hugging the west bank of the Los Angeles River. The crossing sign at Jackson Street *(circle)* appears in the Chaplin frame *(lower left)*.

Charlie is carried to a waiting ambulance from the central plant doorway. The gas compressor plant interior appears in the background.

The ambulance pulls forward, west down Jackson towards Center, past the plant's left doorway.

Harold Lloyd filmed at this same spot 10 years earlier for his 1926 feature, *For Heaven's Sake*. He is attempting to restart his stalled car before a train smashes into it. The arrow points to the partially obscured central doorway appearing in the above frame.

A matching view today.

This vintage aerial view shows the towering natural gas storage tanks near the west bank of the Los Angeles River. The ellipse marks the filming site on Jackson Street. For decades, Los Angeles imposed a 150-foot height limitation for downtown buildings. The lone exception was Los Angeles City Hall (lower left), opened in 1928 and rising 454 feet. Yet the tallest of the three major gas tanks, holding 15 million cubic feet of gas, rose a staggering 378 feet, a conspicuous landmark appearing in dozens of films. The tanks were removed in 1973.

Filming the scene on Jackson Street. Chaplin appears to be pulling the camera.

I discovered this setting by focusing on the upper right corner of this frame enlargement, showing what turned out to be the external crisscross stanchions of a large gas storage tank down the street. Two of the three major gas storage tanks in the area had this crisscross stanchion design. Based on the unique street orientation of each tank, it turned out this tank stood on the northwest corner of Jackson and Center. The rectangle and arrow (above) correspond to the rectangle and arrow in the aerial photo (above left).

LOS ANGELES–
LONG BEACH
HARBORS

B MARINE EXCHANGE
C NAVY LANDING
D FERRY
PASSENGER
& VEHICLE
E YACHT ANCHORAGE

This 1930s map of the Los Angeles–Long Beach Harbor shows settings on Terminal Island that appear in the film: the banana theft scene at Fish Harbor, the wharf set built across from Slip No. 5, Paulette standing across from the Los Angeles Yacht Club, Charlie's shack built along Cerritos Channel, and the So. Cal. Edison power plant. Paul Ayers first made these discoveries. Chaplin filmed *A Busy Day* in Wilmington two blocks west from the point between the "L" and "M" of "WILMING-TON" on the map, while the loading dock in San Pedro ("D" on the map), appears in *A Day's Pleasure*.

Chaplin built an elaborate waterfront set on the northwest corner of Terminal Island across from the opening of Slip No. 5.

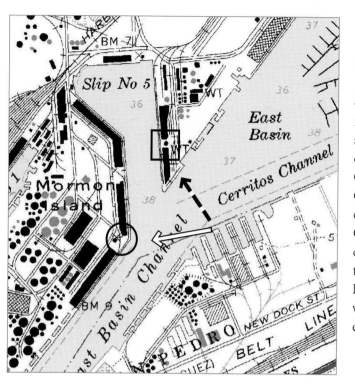

The landscape of Terminal Island is constantly changing. Although this map shows a series of small boat slips at the corner of the Great Basin Channel and Cerritos Channel, the spot was open land at the time Chaplin filmed here. Discussed on the next page, the circle and square highlight two landmark watertowers flanking the entrance to Slip No. 5.

In the far distance of the above shot you can see the north end of Slip No. 5, enlarged here *(left)*. The building to the left is the Coast Fishing Company. The arrow shows the route Buster Keaton drove along Pier A Street in Wilmington, away from the Coast Fishing Company along the north end of Slip No. 5, in his 1929 feature, *Spite Marriage (right)*.

Looking northwest, to the water tower (circle) on the west edge of Slip No. 5, Charlie watches a passing truck. To the far left Berths 177–178 appear in the background.

Charlie works at a dry dock, looking north to the water tower (square) visible behind the scaffolding on the east edge of Slip No. 5.

The central view looks south down Slip No. 5 across the channel towards the spot on Terminal Island where Chaplin filmed. In Buster Keaton's *Spite Marriage*, Buster's character is shanghaied aboard a ship docked at the north end of Slip No. 5. As such, we see the same two water towers looking south (*square and circle*) in the bottom Keaton scenes as we see looking north (*circle and square*) in the top Chaplin scenes.

Chaplin poses at the site of the wharf set on the corner of Terminal Island across from Slip No. 5 to the north in the background. At the far left rooftop across the way you can read "City of Los Angeles, Berth 177-178," while Berths 179-181 appear to the right on the east side of the slip.

Oliver Hardy and a "Bathing Beauty" pass by the same Berths 179-181 *(inset)* in this frame from the 1927 Mack Sennett short, *Crazy to Act*. Hardy would team up with Stan Laurel at the Hal Roach Studios that same year.

Berth 177-178 appears in the background of this rear projection shot of Charlie unintentionally launching a partially constructed ship. The ship is obviously a model.

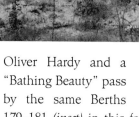

Chaplin's gag echoes one Buster Keaton used 15 years earlier in *The Boat* (1921).

A group of children scramble for the free bananas tossed to them by the "Gamine" (Paulette Goddard) in front of the French Sardine Company, located at Fish Harbor on Terminal Island. The rectangle matches the fish unloading tower in the insert photo of Fish Harbor *(right)*.

The fish-packing industry began here around 1916, and continued to thrive for decades. Star-Kist Foods, Van Camp Sea Foods, and Pan Pacific Fisheries employed as many as 17,000 workers, mostly Japanese, Yugoslavian, Italian, and Portuguese, and berthed 700 tuna boats manned by 5,000 fishermen. Starting in 1906, Japanese-Americans lived in a segregated fishing village near Fish Harbor, growing from 1,000 to 25,000 residents before their forced relocation to World War II internment camps in 1942. The fishing industry slowly declined, the packing plants closed, and today, Fish Harbor stands desolate and barren.

A corresponding view of Fish Harbor today.

This 1930s-era photo shows Fish Harbor bustling with fishing boats.

This vintage shot shows the Los Angeles Yacht Club building on the far side of Cerritos Channel, a bit northeast of the Chaplin waterfront set. Notice the distinctive slender tower.

The Yacht Club appears in yet another scene from Oliver Hardy's 1927 short film, *Crazy to Act*. Here, Hardy has unsurprisingly fallen into Cerritos Channel.

Paulette savors her stolen fruit, with the Yacht Club tower visible across Cerritos Channel in the background *(above and below)*.

Missing the comforts of jail, Charlie consumes a huge cafeteria meal with the goal of being arrested for failing to pay his tab. Here, Charlie seeks a policeman's attention. Below the "CA" of "CAFETERIA" *(left)* you can see the flower girl's shop from *City Lights* across the street, where the heartrending finale *(far right)* was filmed five years earlier.

In a scene cut from the final print, Chaplin attempts to cross a busy city street according to the exacting demands of a traffic cop. This view *(left)* shows the exterior of the cafeteria set featured above, while the corresponding view *(right)* again shows the flower shop set from *City Lights*.

Charlie and Paulette both wind up in a police wagon. This scene was filmed indoors, with stock footage of city streets projected from the rear behind the open door. In this frame *(above)* you can see the Broadway building, at Hollywood Boulevard and Vine, the same department store building where Charlie finds a job later in the film. The same view today appears in the lower right. Built in 1927, the 10-story Renaissance Revival-style building is being converted into luxury condominiums. Its "Broadway Hollywood" rooftop neon sign has been a local landmark since 1931.

Moving further west along Hollywood Boulevard, this rear projection shot now shows the Security Bank building located on the northeast corner of Hollywood and Cahuenga. The same view today appears below. This corner is diagonally opposite from the corner of Hollywood and Cahuenga appearing 22 years earlier in *Tillie's Punctured Romance* (1914).

The Security Bank building (*above*) was the office used by Raymond Chandler's fictional hard-boiled detective, Philip Marlowe. The Hollywood Boulevard entrance of the bank building also appears briefly during a dizzying montage (*above*) as Charlie swoons upon being released from the hospital.

The police wagon carrying Charlie and Paulette spills over, allowing them to escape. David Sameth first located this spot and the dream cottage and department store locations on the next two pages.

This shot was filmed in West Los Angeles looking south down South Sawtelle Boulevard towards the corner of West Massachusetts.

Turning the corner, Charlie and Paulette run east down West Massachusetts from the corner of Sawtelle.

Charlie and Paulette stroll across West Bluffside Drive. Sitting on the grass, they share a domestic fantasy of living in a cozy suburban cottage.

David Sameth found this location searching through old Chaplin records he found at an auction. This scene was filmed on West Bluffside Drive at North Riverton Avenue in Studio City. Although the cottages have been replaced by apartment buildings, the trees and even the crescent-shaped crack in the street asphalt still match up.

Charlie finds work at a department store.

Charlie rushes to tell Paulette the good news that he has landed a job.

The store is the former Broadway Department store, 1645 Vine Street, at the southwest corner of Hollywood Boulevard. The side facing Hollywood Boulevard appears in this scene. This store appears in the background as Charlie and Paulette ride in the paddy wagon *(discussed earlier)*, and as Buster Keaton leaps onto a fire truck running west down Hollywood Boulevard in his 1928 feature, *The Cameraman*.

Charlie greeted Paulette on the Vine side of the building, just down from the corner. Notice the Hollywood Walk of Fame stars now embedded in the sidewalk. The entrance has been enclosed somewhat on each side.

"Of course, it's no Buckingham Palace." Charlie and Paulette survey their new home.

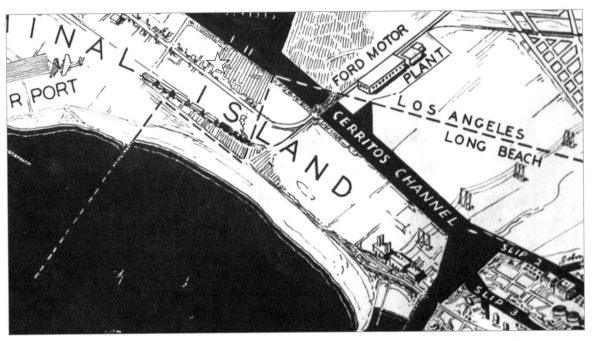

This detail of the harbor map shows the bridge over Cerritos Channel, the Ford assembly plant, and the Edison power plant in relation to where the cabin (*star*) was located.

Charlie leans against the wall of the shack and spills into the water. This view looks south, with the hills of San Pedro and the Palos Verdes peninsula visible in the far background.

This composite image shows in the background the Cerritos Channel, the Ford assembly plant, the "bascule" towers of the Ford Bridge, and the So. Cal. Edison plant at the south end of Terminal Island.

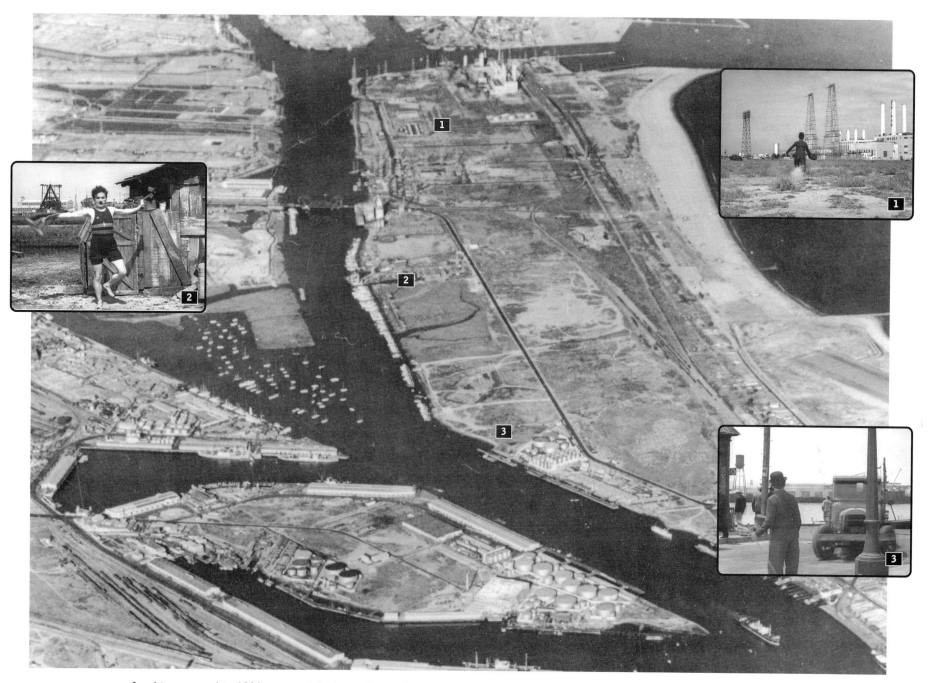

Looking east, this 1930s-era aerial photo shows the area of the wharf set across from Slip No. 5 *(bottom)*; further east, the spot where the shack was situated *(middle)*; and the Edison Plant in the far background *(top)*.

Charlie stretches before a brisk morning swim. The arrow points to the back of a large neon "Ford" sign at the Ford Motor assembly plant.

This vintage aerial view *(right)* shows the Ford Motor assembly plant. The foreground bridge was designed by Joseph Strauss, noted designer of the Golden Gate Bridge in San Francisco. Borrowing concepts from medieval castle drawbridges, the towers (or bascules) used enormous counterweights to raise and lower the bridge span. The Ford Motor plant opened in 1930, employing 2,100 workers at a $6 minimum daily wage. The factory was located on Ford Avenue in Wilmington, ideally situated close to both water and rail transportation.

Charlie dives into a surprisingly shallow stream. Behind him you can see the sign for boat builders Fellows and Stewart.

Eager for a job, Charlie races east towards the So. Cal. Edison power plant. The first plant opened in 1911, and was continuously rebuilt and expanded over the years. A towering landmark, it appears, looking west, in this frame from *Danger Ahead* (1926).

These production stills represent two early scenes from the film: Charlie threatening the matron and Charlie being lead away. Curiously, these stills were not taken at the Ducommun plant location *(circle, below)* where the scenes they depict were actually filmed. Instead, these photos were staged looking toward the northeast corner of Ramirez and Center *(rectangle, below)*, part of the Aliso Street plant appearing towards the end of the film. I was puzzled why the clues in these photos and in the early movie frames contradicted each other until I finally realized that they were taken in different spots.

The early scenes at the Ducommun plant were filmed at Center and Jackson Streets *(circle)*, while the later factory scenes were filmed at the Aliso plant at Ramirez and Howard *(rectangle)*. The opening scene on the Macy Street (Cesar Chavez) Bridge *(star)* was filmed close by.

Charlie leaves the Aliso plant after a strike is called. The view looks east down Ramirez from Howard. The rectangle in the background shows the Ramirez side of the corner building appearing in the rectangle above. The arrow points down Ramirez here and in the photo above.

In this scene the furloughed workers wait to be reassigned their old factory jobs, only to be called back out again on strike. The left view shows the northeast corner of Ramirez and Howard, while the right view, taken from nearly the same spot, shows the southeast corner. A street sign reading Howard and Ramirez appears at the far right. I first discovered this location by matching details off of old aerial photographs and maps.

Looking east, this 1920s aerial view *(left)* shows the Aliso Street gas manufacturing plant. Today, Aliso Street, running at the right edge of the photo, is little more than an access road parallel to the

Hollywood Freeway. Ramirez runs diagonally from the lower left. The unique triangular rooftop trusses appearing in the photo *(upper right)* also appear in this shot from *My Boy* (1921) *(right)* of Jackie Coogan running south down Center Street from Aliso.

Beginning in 1876, the Aliso Street plant manufactured gas from burning coal until the utility converted to pipeline-imported natural gas in 1927. The plant was put in reserve until World War II when it was used to produce butadiene, a synthetic rubber. On July 26, 1943, the Aliso plant's choking smoke and blinding fumes caused the city's first reported smog attack, cutting downtown visibility to three blocks.

Charlie and Paulette pause to rest along the open road *(above)*, and the same view today.

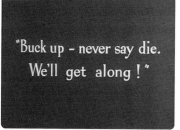

Discouraged, Paulette *(left)* bemoans "What's the use of trying?" Charlie responds "Buck up—never say die. We'll get along!" Arguably, this intertitle signifies the final line of dialog of the silent film era.

Emboldened by Charlie's encouraging words, Charlie and Paulette resume their trek down the open road. This scene was filmed looking west down the Sierra Highway, about two miles west of the final scene location.

These two rare off-camera shots from the collection of Harry Hurwitz, maker of *The Eternal Tramp* documentary, show Chaplin and Paulette filming the penultimate scene. The large assembly of lights, reflectors, and related equipment depict the tremendous advances in filming technology from the single camera-tripod era depicted in *Kid Auto Races at Venice*.

To the melodic strains of Chaplin's most popular musical composition, Charlie encourages Paulette to "Smile."

At the final fade-out, Charlie and Paulette bravely stroll towards their future together beyond the hills. While earlier films conclude with Charlie tramping alone along a dusty road, for the first time, Charlie treads a modern paved highway, arm-in-arm with a companion and female counterpart.

This photo *(lower left)* was taken by Christopher Snowden on nearly the 70th anniversary date of the scene's filming. It was taken looking west down the Sierra Highway at Penman Road, near the town of Acton, nearly 45 miles from the Chaplin Studio. Gerald Smith found this marvelous setting with only the barest of clues. Rollie Totheroh had remembered that this scene was filmed out near Lancaster. Driving around the area, and following hunches, Gerald eventually located the spot. In the process, he discovered the setting on the prior page as well.

Silent cinema is unique among all art forms as having a brief and discrete life span. Overrun by the talkies, silent movies were quickly left behind and they will never return. *Modern Times* was the last major Hollywood-produced film to star a silent film actor in a silent role. This scene therefore not only marks the Little Tramp's final appearance on film, but represents, arguably, the concluding shot of the entire silent film era. As one of silent cinema's pioneers and pre-eminent stars, it is altogether fitting that Chaplin himself should appear in this final scene, bringing down the curtain on the art form he had both established and mastered.

The Great Dictator

Released October 15, 1940

The movie opens with a battle scene from the First World War. The Chaplin Archive's online records indicate Chaplin staged the battle on 21 acres of farm land leased from Christine Malstrom Grace for $150, from between November 22, 1939 to March 21, 1940. David Totheroh located her farm by looking through the old Grantor/Grantee index in the basement of the Hall of Records. The sequence was filmed in Woodland Hills between Chalk Hill to the north and the corner of Wells Drive and Kelvin Avenue to the south. At the time, the community was still named Girard, self-titled by developer Victor Girard Kleinberger, who subdivided the community in the 1920s.

This Google Earth aerial view looking north *(middle)* shows the former Grace property, snuggled into the curved base of Chalk Hill.

This montage *(above right)* looks north to Chalk Hill, a San Fernando Valley landmark, whose ridgeline marks the northern boundary of the Grace property. You can see white chalk-like formations in the side of the hill. At one time, Bob Hope owned the property on the other side of the hill.

This photo is taken from 5028 Dumont Place, looking north to Chalk Hill. The battle sequence was most likely filmed a bit further south and east, but houses and trees almost completely block the view.

Charlie's comic efforts to fire the massive Big Bertha cannon is a highlight of the opening scene. One massive shell merely dribbles out of the cannon mouth, while another only manages to destroy an outhouse a few hundred yards away. The cannon reportedly took two months to build at a cost of $15,000. This view looking west shows the cannon being readied to depart the Chaplin Studio. The rectangle marks part of the set appearing in a later scene, the arrow marks the studio tower. The Big Bertha images are from the Totheroh Family Collection, courtesy of Frank Underwood, son of Chaplin character actor Loyal Underwood.

Big Bertha as it appears in the film.

Big Bertha turns left from La Brea onto De Longpre, the same corner appearing in *A Day's Pleasure (below)*.

Backing Big Bertha through the studio gate onto La Brea.

Chaplin plays dual roles in the film, a Jewish barber and Adenoid Hynkel, the Great Dictator of Tomania. During the opening war scenes, the barber helps a pilot named Schultz to escape the enemy, but later suffers amnesia when their plane crashes. The barber is hospitalized for years while his doppelganger Hynkel rises to power. The barber returns home to find his ghetto neighborhood overrun by storm troopers, and is nearly lynched before Schultz, now a powerful officer, rescues the barber who once saved his life.

As conditions worsen, the ghetto residents escape to neighboring Osterlich, while the barber and Schultz are sent to a concentration camp. Schultz and the barber escape camp wearing stolen army uniforms at the same time that Hynkel is duck hunting in civilian clothes nearby. When Hynkel is mistakenly locked away, the barber, presumed to be Hynkel, is called to speak in his place before a mass rally. The film ends as the barber finds his voice, and pleads for peace, brotherhood, and democracy.

Aside from being an outstanding comedy, *The Great Dictator* is remarkable for a number of reasons. First, it documents one of the most extraordinary coincidences of the 20th century. Chaplin and Hitler, respectively the funniest man in the world and the most reviled, not only shared a passing resemblance, but were born four days apart in April 1889. Next, Chaplin dared to challenge Hitler's tyranny at a time when the United States was still officially neutral. The film was a huge gamble, made possible only because Chaplin owned his own studio and privately financed the production.

Third, although the plot requires the barber character to be Jewish, in many respects he is indistinguishable from the Little Tramp, right down to his moustache, cane, and bowler hat. Thus, despite "retiring" the character in *Modern Times*, arguably the Little Tramp makes his final appearance in this picture. Fourth, the project was Chaplin's first traditional talking film, produced more than a decade after the advent of sound. Considering that the Tramp did not speak (he only sang) in *Modern Times*, the barber's heartfelt oratory concluding the film can be seen as both the Tramp's first and parting words recorded on film.

Finally, the film was a huge success—Chaplin's highest grossing film to date. It was rewarded that year with five Academy Award nominations, not only for Best Picture, but with Chaplin for Best Actor, Jack Oakie for Best Supporting Actor, Meredith Willson for Best Original Score, and Chaplin for Best Original Screenplay.

The scene where Charlie is released from the hospital *(left)* was filmed on the studio lot. The studio screening room door is disguised with a prop "SURGERY" sign. The ellipse in the frame matches the ellipse by the women's dressing room in the aerial photo of the studio *(bottom right)*. A similar view of the dressing rooms from *How to Make Movies* appears bottom left.

The circular rooftop air ducts (*ellipse*) appear in this photo and in the aerial shot below. The assembled extras were used in the subway scene from *Modern Times*.

Charlie and Paulette Goddard stroll north along the ghetto set. The prop billboard (*square*) at the end of the street matches the Big Bertha studio photo two pages back. We can also see the curved roof and circular rooftop air vents of the enclosed shooting stage built where the open-air stage once stood.

The arrow in this aerial view matches the direction of the arrow in the above frame. The open-air stage in the corner has been built over. Another smaller stage has been built where the studio pool once stood between the long row of dressing rooms and the main stages.

Chaplin used the campus of the Harvard Military School for the concentration camp scenes. It was located within the block bounded by West 16th Street (now Venice Boulevard) to the north and Western Avenue to the east. The frame *(right)* is oriented looking to the northwest, while the panorama shot *(below)*, looks to the northeast. The rectangle marks the matching portion of Harvard Hall appearing in both the frame and the photo. In the panorama below we see, from left to right: Junior Hall in the far distance, which contained school rooms; the dormitory Howard Hall in the foreground; Rugby Hall, with the kitchen and dining rooms, in the middle background; and, finally, Harvard Hall at the right. The west side of Harvard Hall, facing the camera, contained a two-story auditorium. In later years the campus was used as a vocational school. Today, an anonymous shopping center and parking lot fills the site.

"Harvard-School" Los Angeles, Cal. May 26th, 1911.

Hollywood Sign

Syd Chaplin took 16mm home movies of his brother Charlie at work during the production. Stitched together, his panning shot taken from the roof of the Chaplin Studio garage shows the width of the back lot. At the far left is the studio gate, and a matching frame of Chaplin entertaining guests several years earlier. Looking up the main street, we see towards the back where Chaplin filmed a motorcade scene, while closer in stands the flower shop set from the *City Lights* finale. The upper right arrow marks the Hollywood sign in the far distance. The front of the street set, at the lower right, is where Chaplin assessed a nude statue in *City Lights*.

The ghetto neighbors flee to Osterlich across a narrow and distinctive bridge *(below)*. Harry Medved, author of *Hollywood Escapes: The Hollywood Guide to Southern California's Great Outdoors*, and Mike Malone suggested clues for locating this bridge. Jeffrey Castel de Oro scouted the area, and found the bridge at the Peter Strauss Ranch *(upper right)*. The bridge crosses Triunfo Creek just east of Troutdale Road.

Mistaken for the escaped barber, Hynkel is taken away by two storm troopers *(lower left)*. Gerald Smith first found this spot. Chaplin filmed this scene at Malibou Lake in the Santa Monica Mountains. This view *(lower center)* looks south from Highpoint Drive at the Lake Vista Bridge crossing the north end of the lake, just south of Paramount Ranch.

This map *(right)* shows the Peter Strauss Ranch, and nearby Malibou Lake along the Mulholland Highway in the Santa Monica Mountains.

Hynkel stages an enormous rally to greet Dictator Benzino Napaloni (played by Jack Oakie). Although filmed inside a soundstage, the baroque dome of the Pasadena City Hall appears as a backdrop. Designed in 1925 by John Bakewell, Jr., and Arthur Brown, the building is located at 100 N. Garfield Avenue at Union Street in Pasadena.

A contemporary newspaper account noted that, like all Chaplin pictures, *The Great Dictator* was written, directed, acted, produced, edited, and scored by Chaplin, who passed on the sets, costumes, and photography as well. With the naïve innocence of that pre-war era, the reporter concludes that when it comes to making movies, Chaplin is himself a great dictator. Chaplin would later recount that had he known the true horrors of the concentration camps at the time, he would not have been able to complete the picture.

Despite its important messages, *The Great Dictator* is filled with wonderful comic sequences, allowing Chaplin to play a Tramp-like character one last time. Its release signaled the end of an amazing arc of comic filmmaking that began with Chaplin's earliest Keystones more than a quarter of a century before. Chaplin had helped to create and master the art of silent film, but he would never again make a silent picture, nor would he ever again appear wearing his Tramp guise on film. By the time Chaplin released his next film, *Monsieur Verdoux*, in 1947, two decades had passed since the advent of sound, and Chaplin's remarkable reign as the world's pre-eminent filmmaker and entertainer had passed.

Afterword

Notes on Time and Technology

Researching this book continuously reminded me of two seemingly opposing forces—time and technology. As the silent movie era becomes increasingly remote in time, technology makes it increasingly accessible. As a young teenager, before the DVD revolution and even before VHS, I had virtually no access to silent era classics aside from reading books, catching an occasional show on public television, and viewing the dozen or so two-reel comedies I had collected on 8mm film. Back then it was unimaginable that I would someday own all of the great works of Charlie Chaplin, Buster Keaton, and Harold Lloyd, and that at modest cost my humble collection would swell to over 200 films.

The advent of DVD technology has also made feasible, for the first time, the research and movie frame analysis that comprise this book. To have accomplished this a generation ago would have required owning physical copies of each film, lugging the reels of film to a photo lab to create photographic prints from the relevant movie frames, and then waiting weeks to retrieve the results. The time, effort, and expense involved would have made such an endeavor nearly impossible.

Today, with DVDs and a home computer, one can compare movie frames from different films almost instantaneously. Thus, not only are classic films more widely available today than ever before, DVD technology also permits us to study these films more closely than previously possible, allowing us to decipher the untold stories of how they were made. For me, knowing *where* Chaplin filmed *Easy Street* makes me feel more connected to the film today, even though I first saw the movie decades ago.

Finally, readers may be surprised to learn that I live hundreds of miles from Los Angeles. Although I visited Los Angeles several times while researching my first book, *Silent Echoes*, with advances in Internet technology it is becoming increasingly irrelevant where one lives. In fact, although I was assisted by generous colleagues living in Los Angeles, I made most of the discoveries in this book on my home computer. The Los Angeles-based photo archives I visited briefly in person while researching *Silent Echoes* are now searchable online. The Sanborn fire insurance maps and historic *Los Angeles Times* newspaper files, once available only on rolls of microfilm, are also now searchable online. And with free Internet services such as Terraserver, Google Earth, Live Local, and A9 Maps, one can type in a Los Angeles street address and instantly retrieve aerial, oblique, and even street level photographs of a selected location.

While nothing replaces the immediacy of visiting a place in person, these amazing Internet tools allow armchair travelers to swoop all over Los Angeles at the click of a button. I have to chuckle that 10 years ago, when I first deduced the location of the church Buster Keaton used in *Seven Chances*, I had to wait six months for my next visit to Los Angeles to confirm that the church was still standing. Years later, within a few seconds of first recognizing the setting of the charity hospital from *The Kid*, I had not only retrieved several vintage photos of the building, but also satellite photos confirming that it is still standing. For film location buffs, the Internet now provides instant virtual gratification.

Select Bibliography

Kiehn, David, *Broncho Billy and the Essanay Film Company*, Farwell Books, 2003.

Mitchell, Glenn, *The Chaplin Encyclopedia*, BT Batsford, 1997; *A to Z of Silent Film Comedy*, BT Batsford, 1998.

Pitt, Leonard and Dale, *Los Angeles A to Z*, University of California Press, 1997.

Robinson, David, *Chaplin: His Life and Art*, McGraw-Hill, 1985.

Stanton, Jeffrey, *Venice California, Coney Island of the Pacific*, Donahue Publishing, 2005.

Favorite Websites

Some highly recommended websites include: Brent Dickerson's award-winning A Visit to Old Los Angeles, which uses vintage post cards to guide you along major city streets at http://www.csulb.edu/~odinthor/socal1.html, Martin Schall's (from Kornwestheim, Germany!) amazing study of Los Angeles architecture, cataloging important buildings from each era, and even indexing them on an interactive map at http://www.you-are-here.com/, Gerald Smith's Chaplin Film Locations Then and Now, a wonderful site for online photos, maps, and other Chaplin resources, and which was the starting point for many discoveries in this book, at http://jerre.com/, and Dr. Lisa Stein's Chaplin fan site: http://www.thelittlefellow.org/.

For vintage photos try the Los Angeles Public Library History Department Photo Collection: http://www.lapl.org/; the USC Digital Archive: http://digarc.usc.edu:8089/cispubsearch/; the California State Library Picture Catalog: http://www.lib.state.ca.us/html/welcome.html; and the Santa Monica Public Library Image Archives: http://www.smpl.org/.

Internet Travel to Chaplin Sites

If you don't live near Los Angeles (and even if you do), you can view the Chaplin film sites with unprecedented ease by visiting a number of free services over the Internet: for satellite views try Google Earth: http://earth.google.com/ or Terraserver: http://terraserver.microsoft.com/; for street level views try A9 Maps: http://maps.a9.com/; and perhaps my favorite, for bird's eye oblique aerial views, try Live Local: http://local.live.com/. With these services you can get real sense of each filming spot, and how it fits in to the surrounding area.

Author Contact

Questions and comments are welcome at John@SilentEchoes.net

Visit **www.SilentEchoes.net** and **www.SilentTraces.net**.

Credits

All images from Chaplin films made from 1918 onwards, copyright © Roy Export Company Establishment. CHARLES CHAPLIN, CHAPLIN, and the LITTLE TRAMP, photographs from and the names of Mr. Chaplin's films are trademarks and/or service marks of Bubbles Incorporated SA and/or Roy Export Company Establishment. Used with permission. Essanay and Mutual Chaplin images reproduced courtesy of David Shepard and Film Preservation Associates.

Photo Credits

Association Chaplin, cover center and left, 108 upper right, 110 center, 155 both aerial, 158 both left, 161 both left, 162 lower right, 164 top and lower left, 165 lower left, 180 upper right lower left, 185 upper right, 186 upper right, lower center, 191 upper right, 204 upper right and center, 206 upper left, 207 lower left, 210 all right, 211 lower left, 230 lower right, 236 lower right, 237 top center, 238 lower left, 239 upper left, 242 lower left, 246 upper left, lower right, 248 all, 249 both left, 250 upper right, lower left, 251 upper right, 252 right, 253 lower right, 254 all, 255 all, 256 upper right, 257 upper right, 262 all, 263 all, 264 lower right, 265 middle top, 269 lower left, 271 both left, 273 upper left, 285 upper left, 286 both top, right, 292 lower right, 293 all, 295 center, 301.

Totheroh Family Collection, cover right, 170, 171 upper left.

Seaver Center for Western History Research, Los Angeles County Museum of Natural History, 6, 135 top, 165 upper left, 202 lower left, 221 lower right.

UCLA Air Photo Archives, Department of Geography, Spence Air Photo Collection, 13, 32 lower right, 106 bottom, 137 upper right, 215 lower right.

Marc Wanamaker—Bison Archives, 14, 54 both left, 58, 65 upper left, 79 upper right, 80 top, 113, 114, 116 bottom, 117 upper left, 118 both, 119 lower right, 132 upper right, lower left, 146, 147 lower right, 149 lower left, 171 lower right, 178 right, 197 upper left, 216, 244 bottom.

Brent Walker, 15, 27 lower left, 39 both right, 44 lower right, 51 right, 132 lower right, 209 right center.

California Historical Society, Title Insurance and Trust Photo Collection, Department of Special Collections, University of Southern California, 10, 16, 19, 21 top, 22 upper left, 23 lower left, 26 both, 27 both right, 30 right inset, 32 top, 35 lower left, 37, 39 upper left, 41 lower left, 42 lower right, 46 upper right, 47 both left, 49 upper right, 50 lower right, 51 bottom, 53 upper right, 57 top, bottom, 79 lower right, 80 bottom, 81, 84 upper right, 87 upper right, 88 bottom, 89 upper right, 90 lower left, 91 left, 92 all, 93 lower right, 94 lower right, 95 lower right, 98, 103 right, 104 lower right, 106 upper left, 107 upper right, 111 bottom, 126 both right, 129 middle, 133 all, 134 bottom, 139 lower right, 140 lower left, 141 left, 144 upper right, lower left, 169 lower right, 173 lower right, 176 bottom, 182 upper right, 183 both right, 184 two upper right, 185 lower left, 187 lower right, 194 lower right, 196, 198 lower left, 200 lower right, 203 all photos, 214 lower right, 220 left, 224 top, 225 upper left, 226 upper right, 229, 269 upper left, 274 both right, 278 upper right, 285 lower left.

Jeffrey Castel De Oro, 17 top, 20 all, 21 lower right, 22 lower right, 25 lower right, 29 lower left, 30 lower left, 34 upper right, 45 both bottom, 47 lower right, 57 lower right, 82 upper right, 99 both right, 104 upper right, 105 bottom, 129 bottom left and right, 134 upper middle, 140 lower right, 141 upper right, 142 lower right, 156 lower right, 164 lower right, 168 bottom, 169 upper right, 182 lower right, 188 right, 189 bottom, 190 upper right, 209 lower right, 223 lower left, 225 lower left, 226 lower right, 227 both right, 249 both right, 259 lower right, 265 upper right, 267 upper right, 268 lower right, 279 all right, 296 upper right, lower left.

The Douris Corporation, David Shepard, Film Preservation Associates, and Kino International Corporation, 23 upper right, 46 upper left, 52 upper right, 77 upper right, 84 lower left, 96 lower right, 107 lower right, 108 lower left, 109 top, 110 middle left, lower left, 111 top, frames 1, 2, 3, and 5, 117 middle and top right, 120 both bottom, 121 lower right, 122 all bottom, 123 lower

right, 124 bottom two right, 131 lower left, 135 lower right, 181 bottom, 199 lower right, 205 center and lower right, 209 all left, 212 middle and lower right, 218 both right, 219 lower right, 245 upper right, 247 both right, 260 lower right, 265 lower right, 273 lower right.

Lobster Films, 23 lower right, 82 upper left, 97 both right, 174 upper right, lower left, 203 lower right, 273 right, 275 lower left.

Security Pacific National Bank Photograph Collection/Los Angeles Public Library, 24, 25 both top, 28, 29 top, 30 lower right, 31 top, 33 top, 39 lower left, 42 lower right, 52 lower right, 82 lower left, 86, 87 lower right, 89 lower left, 90 upper left, 107 both left, 112 upper left, 138 top, 147 upper left, 150, 154 right, 160 upper right, 175 both left, 182 lower left, 191 lower left, 193, 195, 197 upper right, 198 upper right, 211 upper left, 212 top, 228 upper right, 233 upper right, lower left, 270, 275 upper left, 277 upper right, 282 upper right, 283, 286 lower left.

El Pueblo de Los Angeles Historical Monument, 31 bottom, 112 lower left, 134 right, 136 upper left, lower right, 137 upper left, 138 bottom, 169 lower left, 212 bottom.

Brent Dickerson, 32 left.

Florence Ung Francis Collection: Chinese American Museum/El Pueblo de Los Angeles Historical Monument, 34 upper left, lower right, 35 lower right, 36, 102, 110 both top, 198 lower right, 201, 202 upper left, lower right, 213 lower left, 215 upper right, lower left.

David Shepard and Film Preservation Associates, 33 lower right, 35 upper right, 43 middle left, both center, 53 center, 106 upper right, 141 bottom three, 184 lower left, 228 both bottom, 284 lower right.

Jeffrey Vance Collection, 38 top, 120 top, 122 top, 145 upper left, 154 lower left, 163 lower right, 166 lower right, 230 lower left, 285 upper right.

Los Angeles Times Copyright 1939, page 38, Copyright 1938, page 105, page 233. Reprinted with permission.

Library of Congress, 40 bottom, 179 top, 205 lower left, 234 bottom, 294 bottom.

U.S. Geologic Survey, 43 upper right, 251 upper left, 271 upper right.

Laughsmith Entertainment Inc., 43 lower left, 44 lower left, 50 both top, 54 lower right, 94 left, 181 left, 204 lower right.

Martin Schall, 46 center, 48 both right, 53 lower right.

Harold Lloyd Entertainment, Inc., 49 both bottom, 51 left, 84 middle left, 94 top, 104 lower left, 135 bottom, 148 bottom both, 149 upper left, 168 right, 169 upper left, 224 middle, 268 lower left.

Marilyn Slater, 50 lower left, 56 lower left.

Bruce Torrence Historical Collection, 55, 117 bottom, 124 left.

Dr. Lisa Stein, 56 lower right, 119 lower left, 125 upper right, 214 lower left, 256 lower right.

David Kiehn, 61 all, 64, 66 lower left, 67 bottom, 69 lower left, 70 upper right, lower left, 71 center, 100, 101.

Jill M. Singleton and Philip Holmes, 67 center.

Gerald Smith, 68 both top, 73 lower left, 74 both right, 239 lower left, 241 lower left.

Charles Allen Dealey Family collection, 64, 69 upper left.

Sam Gill, 69 upper right.

San Francisco History Center, San Francisco Public Library, 73 upper right, 75, 76 all, 77 upper left, lower right.

Bruce Bengtson, 77 lower left.

Santa Monica Public Library Image Archives, 83 lower right, 84 right, 148 upper left, 242 lower right, 243 left.

David Raptka, 89 upper left.

Larry Stefan and Richard M. Roberts of the Slaphappy Collection, 89 lower right, 135 lower left, 197 both bottom, 205 center right.

California History Room, California State Library, Sacramento, California, 91 lower right, 99 left, 105 upper left, 129 upper right, 223 upper right, 258 lower right, 266 left.

David Shepard, Film Preservations Associates, Serge Bromberg, and Lobster Films, 96 bottom middle, 204 lower left, 237 lower right.

Christopher Snowden, UnknownVideo.com, 102 upper left right, 287 lower right, 288 upper right, 289 lower left.

Turner Entertainment, 109 lower right, 111 far right, 211 lower right, 271 lower right, 272 lower left, lower right.

Shunichi Ohkubo, 119 both top.

The Academy of Motion Picture Arts and Sciences, 123 left, 199 left.

Los Angeles Fire Department Historical Society Archive, 125 lower right.

Paul R. Ayers, 130 all right, 177 bottom, 180 lower right, 220 right, 221 upper right, 222 both right, 250 lower right, 251 bottom, 274 lower left.

Dr. Frank Scheide, 131 lower right.

Kenneth & Gabrielle Adelman, California Coastal Records, 143 upper right, 145 lower right.

David Totheroh, 143 bottom, 144 lower right, 145 upper right, 171 lower left, 240 both left, upper right, 290 bottom.

Jeff Stanton, 149 right middle, 245 lower right.

Kevin Brownlow, Photoplay Productions, Ltd., 155 upper left, 159 upper right, 160 lower right, 175 right, 209 upper right, 237 top center, 256 lower left.

The Jim Henson Company, 156 upper left.

Bill Roddy, http://americahurrah.com/, 173 middle left.

Robert S. Birchard Collection, 174 lower right.

Mary Sue Roberts, 184 lower right.

Occidental College Archives and Special Collections, 189 both top, 190 upper left.

Pictometry International, 190 bottom.

June Ahn, 192 lower right.

David Sameth, 200 left, 280 bottom.

The Bancroft Library, University of California, Berkeley, 215 upper left, lower left, 272 lower center.

Ralph Melching Collection, Pacific Railroad Museum/Pacific Railroad Society, San Dimas, California, 217 lower right, 219 upper left.

Automobile Club of Southern California Archives, 232 upper right.

Santa Clarita Valley Historical Society, 232 lower right.

Charles Seims, 234 top.

Sugar Bowl Ski Resort, 239 right, 240 lower right, 241 lower right.

Dana Scanlon, 241 upper left.

Norm Sayler, 241 upper right.

Hal Roach Studios, 244 upper right, 266 lower right, 267 lower right.

Bryant Arnett, 259 lower right, 261 lower left.

The Historical Society of Long Beach, 284 upper right.

Harry Hurwitz Collection, 288 both bottom.

Google Earth™, 290 center.

Totheroh Family collection courtesy of Frank Underwood, 291 all.

Kristin Bengtson, back cover, lower left.

All remaining photos were taken by the author or are from the author's collection. Every effort has been made to secure permission and provide appropriate credit; the author regrets any inadvertent errors, and would be happy to insert appropriate acknowledgments in subsequent editions of the book.

Chaplin, the center of attention, invites closer inspection, as if sitting beneath a giant magnifying glass. Chaplin's unique humor and humanity continue to draw us in. Decades later, the silent traces of his footsteps remain.

If You Like Silent Traces, You'll *Love* Silent Echoes!

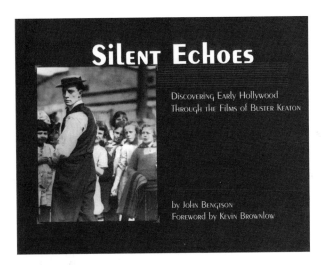

"Mind-boggling . . . What John Bengtson has done is nothing short of remarkable: a deft combination of detective work, archeology, and film buffery. I can't get enough of it!"   —LEONARD MALTIN, film critic and historian

"This is a cinematic and photographic detective story of the first order. Time and artifice have been stripped away. What's left is a wonderful portrait of a city, its principal industry, and one of its best artists."

—KEN BURNS, author/director, *The Civil War, Baseball, Jazz*, etc.

Silent Echoes: Discovering Early Hollywood Through the Films of Buster Keaton is an epic look at a genius at work and at a Hollywood that no longer exists. Painstakingly researching the locations used in Buster Keaton's classic silent films, author John Bengtson combines images from Keaton's movies with archival photographs, historic maps, and scores of dramatic "then" and "now" photos. In the process, Bengtson reveals dozens of locations that lay undiscovered for nearly 80 years.

$24.95
Trade Paper
ISBN 1-891661-06-X
232 pages
11 × 8½
Hundreds of Black-and-White Photographs
Film

Books Available from Santa Monica Press

www.santamonicapress.com • 1-800-784-9553

American Hydrant
by Sean Crane
176 pages $24.95

Atomic Wedgies, Wet Willies & Other Acts of Roguery
by Greg Tananbaum and Dan Martin
128 pages $11.95

The Bad Driver's Handbook
Hundreds of Simple Maneuvers to Frustrate, Annoy, and Endanger Those Around You
by Zack Arnstein and Larry Arnstein
192 pages $12.95

The Butt Hello
and other ways my cats drive me crazy
by Ted Meyer
96 pages $9.95

Calculated Risk
The Extraordinary Life of Jimmy Doolittle
by Jonna Doolittle Hoppes
360 pages $24.95

Can a Dead Man Strike Out?
Offbeat Baseball Questions and Their Improbable Answers
by Mark S. Halfon
192 pages $11.95

Captured!
Inside the World of Celebrity Trials
by Mona Shafer Edwards
Text by Jody Handley
184 pages $24.95

Creepy Crawls
A Horror Fiend's Travel Guide
by Leon Marcelo
384 pages $16.95

Dogme Uncut
Lars von Trier, Thomas Vinterberg and the Gang That Took on Hollywood
by Jack Stevenson
312 pages $16.95

Elvis Presley Passed Here
Even More Locations of America's Pop Culture Landmarks
by Chris Epting
336 pages $16.95

Exotic Travel Destinations for Families
by Jennifer M. Nichols and Bill Nichols
360 pages $16.95

Footsteps in the Fog
Alfred Hitchcock's San Francisco
by Jeff Kraft and Aaron Leventhal
240 pages $24.95

French for Le Snob
Adding Panache to Your Everyday Conversations
by Yvette Reche
400 pages $16.95

Haunted Hikes
Spine-Tingling Tales and Trails from North America's National Parks
by Andrea Lankford
372 pages $16.95

How to Speak Shakespeare
by Cal Pritner and Louis Colaianni
144 pages $16.95

Jackson Pollock: Memories Arrested in Space
by Martin Gray
216 pages $14.95

James Dean Died Here
The Locations of America's Pop Culture Landmarks
by Chris Epting
312 pages $16.95

The Keystone Kid
Tales of Early Hollywood
by Coy Watson, Jr.
312 pages $24.95

L.A. Noir
The City as Character
by Alain Silver and James Ursini
176 pages $19.95

Loving Through Bars
Children with Parents in Prison
by Cynthia Martone
216 pages $21.95

Marilyn Monroe Dyed Here
More Locations of America's Pop Culture Landmarks
by Chris Epting
312 pages $16.95

Movie Star Homes
by Judy Artunian and Mike Oldham
312 pages $16.95

My So-Called Digital Life
2,000 Teenagers, 300 Cameras, and 30 Days to Document Their World
by Bob Pletka
176 pages $24.95

Offbeat Museums
The Collections and Curators of America's Most Unusual Museums
by Saul Rubin
240 pages $19.95

A Prayer for Burma
by Kenneth Wong
216 pages $14.95

Quack!
Tales of Medical Fraud from the Museum of Questionable Medical Devices
by Bob McCoy
240 pages $19.95

Redneck Haiku
Double-Wide Edition
by Mary K. Witte
240 pages $11.95

Route 66 Adventure Handbook
Expanded Third Edition
by Drew Knowles
384 pages $16.95

The Ruby Slippers, Madonna's Bra, and Einstein's Brain
The Locations of America's Pop Culture Artifacts
by Chris Epting
312 pages $16.95

School Sense: How to Help Your Child Succeed in Elementary School
by Tiffani Chin, Ph.D.
408 pages $16.95

Silent Echoes
Discovering Early Hollywood Through the Films of Buster Keaton
by John Bengtson
232 pages $24.95

Silent Traces
Discovering Early Hollywood Through the Films of Charlie Chaplin
by John Bengtson
304 pages $24.95

Tiki Road Trip
A Guide to Tiki Culture in North America
by James Teitelbaum
288 pages $16.95

	Quantity	Amount
American Hydrant ($24.95)	_____	_____
Atomic Wedgies, Wet Willies & Other Acts of Roguery ($11.95)	_____	_____
The Bad Driver's Handbook ($12.95)	_____	_____
The Butt Hello . . . and Other Ways My Cats Drive Me Crazy ($9.95)	_____	_____
Calculated Risk ($24.95)	_____	_____
Can a Dead Man Strike Out? ($11.95)	_____	_____
Creepy Crawls ($16.95)	_____	_____
Dogme Uncut ($16.95)	_____	_____
Elvis Presley Passed Here ($16.95)	_____	_____
Exotic Travel Destinations for Families ($16.95)	_____	_____
Footsteps in the Fog: Alfred Hitchcock's San Francisco ($24.95)	_____	_____
French for Le Snob ($16.95)	_____	_____
Haunted Hikes ($16.95)	_____	_____
How to Speak Shakespeare ($16.95)	_____	_____
Jackson Pollock: Memories Arrested in Space ($14.95)	_____	_____
James Dean Died Here: America's Pop Culture Landmarks ($16.95)	_____	_____
The Keystone Kid: Tales of Early Hollywood ($24.95)	_____	_____
L.A. Noir: The City as Character ($19.95)	_____	_____

	Quantity	Amount
Loving Through Bars ($21.95)	_____	_____
Marilyn Monroe Dyed Here ($16.95)	_____	_____
Movie Star Homes ($16.95)	_____	_____
My So-Called Digital Life ($24.95)	_____	_____
Offbeat Museums ($19.95)	_____	_____
A Prayer for Burma ($14.95)	_____	_____
Quack! Tales of Medical Fraud ($19.95)	_____	_____
Redneck Haiku ($9.95)	_____	_____
Route 66 Adventure Handbook ($16.95)	_____	_____
The Ruby Slippers, Madonna's Bra, and Einstein's Brain ($16.95)	_____	_____
School Sense ($16.95)	_____	_____
Silent Echoes: Early Hollywood Through Buster Keaton ($24.95)	_____	_____
Silent Traces ($24.95)	_____	_____
Tiki Road Trip ($16.95)	_____	_____

Shipping & Handling:
1 book $4.00
Each additional book is $1.00

Subtotal _____
CA residents add 8.25% sales tax _____
Shipping and Handling (see left) _____
TOTAL _____

Name _____

Address _____

City _____ State _____ Zip _____

☐ Visa ☐ MasterCard Card No.:_____

Exp. Date _____ Signature _____

☐ Enclosed is my check or money order payable to:

Santa Monica Press LLC
P.O. Box 1076
Santa Monica, CA 90406